Praise for F. Scott Ser

Playing Soldier

"...a gripping memoir of life, war, loss, and recovery that effectively conveys the fear and horror of a shell-shocked veteran who had once romanticized the idea of being a soldier." —*IndieReader*

"Vividly written, honest, and often deeply disturbing, readers on finishing this book will be asking if war is ever truly worth it. A Wishing Shelf recommended read!" —*The Wishing Shelf*

"*Playing Soldier* is truly a book for everyone. There are pages that will never let go of you. What real writing is supposed to do." —*Baron Wormser, author of Tom o'Vietnam*

"...strikingly profound." —*N.N. Light's Book Heaven*

"An honest, powerful and expertly crafted read." —*Pacific Book Review*

"Rarely does a memoir feel this raw and immediate." —*Self-Publishing Review*

"...a savagely honest work, unadulterated by too much self-editing or posturing." —*The Independent Review of Books*

"His luminous, illustrative prose paints vivid word-pictures..." —*Booklife*

Also by F. Scott Service

Lines in the Sand (An American Soldier's Personal Journey in Iraq)
Playing Soldier (A Chronicle of Spiritual Awakening)

an asylum tap dance

the Book of Jack

F. SCOTT SERVICE

1st edition

ISBN (Paperback): 979-8-9934822-2-4

Library of Congress Control Number: 2025922141

Publisher: F. Scott Service (www.fscottservice.com)
Editing: The Wishing Shelf and F. Scott Service
Cover Design: F. Scott Service
Typesetting and Interior Design: Euan Monaghan
Author Photograph: Melissa Hartigan Photography

Printed on demand in the United States of America and throughout the world

This is a work of creative nonfiction and is not meant to be an annal. It is a collection of memories and expressions, in feeling, of a life spent with my best friend. As close as these events are to my heart, memory is often subjective, partial, and provides for a fictive aspect however true the stories may be.

Further, the political, social, and cultural opinions, observations, and/or speculations expressed in this work are solely those of me (the author) and do not necessarily reflect fact. I do not make any guarantee for the correctness and/or completeness of that information.

Additionally, in no way do I represent the companies, corporations, or brands mentioned in this book and the likeness of historical/famous figures have been used fictitiously. I do not speak for or represent these people. Unless otherwise indicated, all the names in this book have been changed accordingly to protect the privacy and/or anonymity of individuals.

Finally, this book deals with suicide, substance use/abuse, domestic violence, and other personal matters. While I have taken great lengths to ensure the subject matter is dealt with in a compassionate and respectful manner, it may be troubling for some readers.

Discretion is advised.

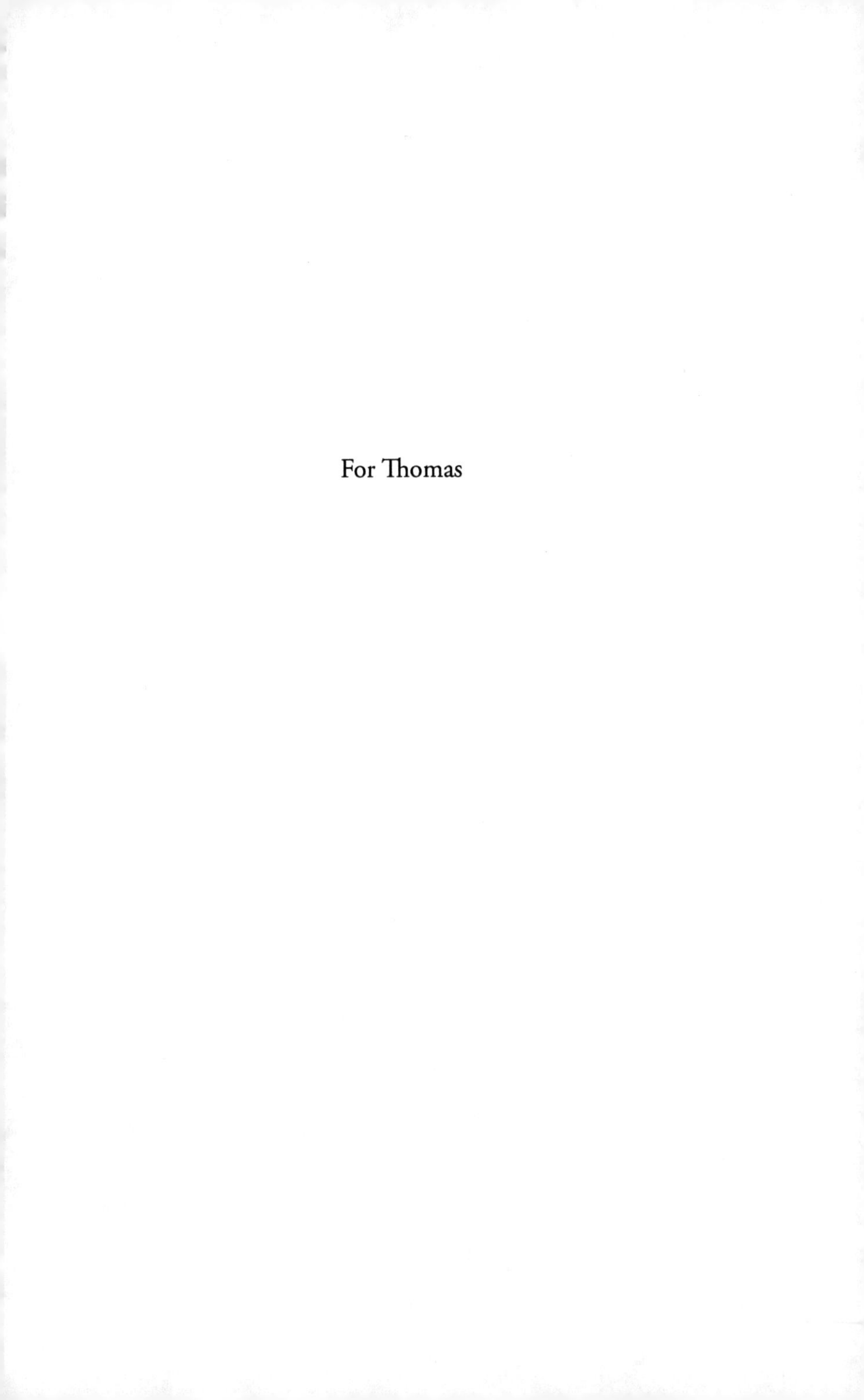

For Thomas

an asylum tap dance

the Book of Jack

Chapters

When we can't dream any longer we die.

—Emma Goldman

Barrels of Fun

Completely unaware when it happened, I was caught with my fly open.

And so surprised by the deep, resonant voice of the law, dribble bathed my thighs, dampening my blue jeans.

Late that early spring night, it was past midnight in the familiar stomping grounds of our small town amid New England's hills and forests. A borough born in the 18th century during the original colonial, pioneered days of America. Founded by those transplanted pilgrims from Europe who survived the early years thanks to the generosity of Indigenous people.

They scantly perceived what was to come.

A lot of life seems to happen when it's least expected.

Now, our hamlet has merged with a state university. A sprawling marriage of both eager faces who look to their future, and families who nest on side streets. With neighbors who wave and mow their lawns; who wash their cars and walk their dogs.

Familial.

We had a couple of grocery stores. A hardware store down the street from the movie theater. A beauty salon next to the community co-op and bakery. A fruit and vegetable stand owned by a local farmer. A garage, where everyone knew the mechanic by name. And he knew them. Liquor stores. A pharmacy. And of course, a church. A slow-paced, almost demure community for the people who worked hard for retirement while rearing children in the hope they would someday be like the 'lucky kids' up on campus.

We were two of those lucky kids.

A life of opportunity in front of us.

And on this school night, we were behind the local 7-11, well into our twelve pack of bribed Budweiser. The source of our late night suds? Hush money tucked into the palm of a wannabe academic on his four-year visit. A short-term, transient pupil and resident. They came and went all the time, but they served as a convenience. A never-ending supply of enablers as they took our five extra bucks and handed us the prize. The result? Eternal, carefree vagabonds with our own private soiree while everyone else slept.

And he was in the middle of a ramble. His mind and his mouth on the go—as was always the case. As he had for as long as my sixteen-year-old mind would allow.

Jack.

The gregarious, lively spirited intellectual who never failed to entertain me with innovative ideas and limitless imagination.

Jack.

The maverick oddball who plunged into wild, zestful, yet somehow, deliberate and substantial directions, within his trail-blazing mind.

Jack.

My chatterbox best friend.

But my attention was elsewhere. The relief that flooded through me was too exquisite to let go of as I exhaled with satisfaction while Jack's soliloquy faded into the background. I never noticed the alternated hues of the reds and blues as they flashed on the gray, wood wall I faced, putting my watery infraction on stark display. As they danced on the small, newly built wooden deck attached to the back delivery entrance of the store where Jack sat, his legs casually swinging over the side.

"Am I going to need some backup here?" the voice boomed.

The moon shone dimly through puffy clouds, and only the summer song of crickets responded as Jack's ramble abruptly stopped. But hardly a few seconds passed before he recovered. Even when drunk, his speech and manner was steady, clear, and I was always grudgingly impressed by this talent of his. A feat I was never able to master.

"Good evening, officer. What seems to be the trouble?" asked Jack.

Like a cow caught in a thunderstorm, I stood there, my head swiveled in frothy bathed, light-headed torpor.

"Zip it up, kid," continued the tone of authority. "Then come here, both of you."

"Okay," I managed, turning away as my fingers fiddled with the front of my jeans.

Jack slid off the deck and scooped up his can of Budweiser. Together, with Jack more cavalier, we approached the car and the local arm of the law. The college cop leaned back on the front of the hood, the beam from his Maglite shining directly on us. I caught a glimpse of a smirk hewed on his chiseled face.

"Been doing a little drinking tonight, I see," proclaimed the tongue of command.

I shrugged, my attempt at a casual feign lost in blindness, the light so bright, my eyes hurt, begging to close.

"Just a little," grinned Jack.

"And I'm betting you're a bit too young for that."

"Just a little," repeated Jack, his fingers raised and pinched together.

I caught a glimmer of what was now a full-blown smile as the local badge swung his light to the 7-11, then back to us. "But old enough to know better about urinating on public property."

"That was me, officer," I said, "Jack had nothing—"

"Put a clamp on it, kid," ordered the flatfoot. A pause. "I *should* bust you. Handcuff you and throw you both in the back of my car."

"Shit," said Jack.

"I ought to make you the town spectacle. I can see the local headline now - local numbnuts busted with pants halfway down."

"You're right, officer," answered a now humble Jack. "That would be us."

The seconds ticked by, and I suspected the cop was enjoying keeping us in suspense. Then, "I'll make you a deal," he proposed.

"Anything," I breathed. My hope, however fruitless and laughable at this point, was that he couldn't smell our breaths.

"You pour out the rest of what you have, all of it, not just what's in your hand, and get out of here. But I never want to see you back here again. Understand?"

"Right you are, officer. Won't happen. Not us. You have my word on it," said a renewed, cheerful Jack.

Six beers splashed onto the dirt. And after Jack, naturally, asked all about his route, the hours he worked, the type of pistol he carried, and where he got his training, the officer, through an increasingly amused grin, waved us off and got back into his car.

"Remember, I don't want to see you back here, boys," the forgiving officer declared from the open window.

"Don't worry. Have a good night, sir," said a relieved Jack, as we rounded the corner of the store, grateful to be out of the spotlight. We walked past the front, and through the empty parking lot. At the intersection of his road and the main road that wound in and through town, we stopped under the fluorescence of a single streetlight. Just us, under a pale, white oasis. Surrounded by the still night and the sound of the crickets, I could hear a car somewhere off in the distance. We never saw the cop leave.

"Well, that was barrels of fun. Whattya wanna do next?" he asked.

I shrugged. "It's late, Jack. We gotta get up for school."

"Horse pucky. The night is young. We're young." He paused. "I know. We could go down to the school bus depot for another raid on the fire extinguishers."

"Jack, that was ages ago. When we were eleven. When we were kids. We're too old for stupid crap like that now. Besides, I almost blinded you with my little good, the bad, and the ugly Clint Eastwood stunt."

"Oh, yeah. Well, not to worry, I can see now."

"Thank God. But no thanks."

I pulled out my pack of Camel's and lit one, then passed it to Jack. Another one for me.

"Anyway, as I was saying before we were so rudely interrupted, I think we should go west, head out on the highway. It would be worth exploring, and the list of places to see is endless once you get by the Great Plains. I'm sure it would fuel your imagination."

"That's cool. I think it'd be a trip. Maybe we could buy that eighteen-wheeler and go into business together."

"We should. We've been talking about that for a long time now. You're good with geography; you memorized that map of the country."

"And played with your Hess truck. What were we? Nine?"

"About that. No time like the present, no time to lose - well, when we graduate anyway. I can't wait to get the fuck out of here." He put his arm around my shoulders and took a drag off his smoke. "Life is short, my friend. We have to go live it."

"Let's talk about it later, Jack," I shrugged. "We have all the time in the world."

"Sounds good. See you tomorrow for some java before school." He turned, crossed the main road, and as he began to disappear up his own, I heard his voice filter through the darkness. "Go west, young man."

"Who's that?" I called.

"Horace Greeley. He was referring to America's manifest destiny."

That's you, Jack, I thought. *Always ready to roll, even with a history lesson.*

"Lookin' for adventure?" I asked.

"Steppenwolf. Now you're gettin' it," he replied cheerfully.

Then, he was gone.

The Worst Joke Ever Told

"Jack's dead, Dana."

"What?"

"He's dead," repeats the distant voice.

Silence.

"Okay, Libby, I gotta tell ya, that's some kind of fucked up sense of humor."

"I'm not joking, Dana. He's gone."

A pause.

"I – I don't understand. Really, what's happened?"

"No one seems to know yet, but I do know he did it this past weekend, sometime on Saturday or Sunday."

"Did *what*?"

"He shot himself."

From the other end of the line, those stark three words rebound through the house on the winding road. The house on top of a short hill surrounded by oaks, birch, and hemlock. With the swamp in the back woods. The neatly placed trash and recycle bins by the side of the driveway. And the tall, bushy Rhododendron out front—big, ruffled white blooms with little stalks capped in yellow. The house where I grew up. Where Jack and I spent so much time—sleepovers, birthday parties, cub scout meetings with snipe hunts, movies, and backyard campouts.

Where we talked for hours about our imagined dreams.

Now, the house is dark except for a soft, mosaic glow emanating from one window. A glow stealing its way through the black grass of night. Overseen by the pale gaze from a nearly full moon.

Icy and prickly.

"Jack – shot – himself?"

"Yeah, he did. I'm so sorry, Dana."

"But I just talked to him. How do you know?"

"Avery told me, and I told her I'd tell you."

The phone almost slips from my hand, my mind calculating through a growing fog. "But it's Tuesday."

"Yes."

"How come I'm just finding out now?"

"It took me a little bit to find you."

Skepticism feels more rational than truth to me. I'm having a hard time feeling the floor underneath my socks. White? Cotton? Are those toes moving?

"He didn't call me," I murmur, more to myself than Libby.

"He didn't call anyone. Well, that's not exactly true. Avery has been looking through his phone records and he made a whole bunch of calls the week before. But not to anyone he was close to. He didn't call Avery, their mom—"

"Joan."

"Yes. Nor me. And apparently not you."

"Why?"

"I don't know. I know he'd been having some problems."

"Yeah, I get that, but those things pass."

"*We* know that."

Fingers tingling.

My heart's beginning to pound.

"Jack's dead?"

"Yes."

The kitchen is swimming and my eyes are blurring. Darkening. Dizzy, I steady myself by grasping the edge of the sink. A blank stare. No feeling. Then turning, I slump to the floor. Slow. In a daze. My eyes wide open, my back resting against the cabinet, my legs spread open. One hand palm up, resting on the cool, gray-colored, tile floor.

Helpless and lifeless.

"Jack's – dead," I whisper.

An immobilizing, yet overwhelming urge to run.

To hide.

"He is, Dana."

"Umm, okay, Libby? I – I have to go. I – umm, need to go now, okay? Okay. I gotta go. I just need to go. Really. I gotta go."

The kitchen disappears. The house disappears. The street disappears. And the world is gone. I recognize the familiar nether world of distant floating; of drifting through post-traumatic stress as it overcomes my body. Only this time it's a new pain. A pinprick of a hole appears in my heart, then, with unbearable slowness, it widens to a gaping, black cavity. Now a tunnel. And I feel myself walking into it. A steady stride as I'm neither here nor there.

As I'm bleeding out in the enveloping emptiness.

"It's okay. I understand. Really."

"Can we – is it alright if we talk later?"

"Of course. I'd like that."

"Okay. Good. I have to go; right now, Libby. I really need to go."

"Call me soon, okay?"

"I will."

Click.

And I'm left adrift in the silence.

Dead Man's Hand

Johnny Cash's "A Boy Named Sue" pierced the tasteless air.

Hot, dry summer air with no conditioning.

Faintly musty and stagnant through the one-floor watering hole.

The saloon, where we had decided to chow down on some grub, was adorned with a covered porch and fake horse railings out in the parking lot. Enclosed by aged walnut-colored, wood-paneled walls and crowded with empty, round, cockeyed tables. Populated with scratched chairs that creaked and Coca-Cola Tiffany lamps which hung with tired spirit. An old billiards table with frayed felt gathered dust in the shadows. And an unclouded sun filtered through the aged, single paned, double hung windows and shone brightly on the grime-laden Mustang parked out front.

In South Dakota.

We sat in a booth in the corner, overseen by a splotched, sepia photo of Wild Bill Hickock. Captured, with his wide-brimmed hat, behind the glass of an ornate, silver lattice frame. His curly, long hair draped down to his shoulders. And a caption:

THE LEGENDARY OUTLAW IN HIS PRIME

CIRCA 1876

His gaze steady with perceptive resignation, Wild Bill looked as if he knew he was living on borrowed time. And he looked bored. Old. Worn out from his years of living with danger. All the years when he lived fast and hard. Killed men and loved women. And fondled one too many aces and eights.

The Dead Man's Hand.

Jack had ordered a steak with baked potato and without an assuming word, when it landed, wolfed it down with incredibly huge bites. He hardly chewed, intent on the job as if a Civil War six gun was pressed to his head.

As my fork hovered above my plate of barely eaten, sauteed, cowboy pork chops, I couldn't help but watch with awe. Like everything else he had chosen to do in his life, he was enthusiastic. So voracious. So vigorous.

And truly vivacious.

I speared a broccoli floret and sat back in the faux leather booth with a warm grin. For the first time in our life together, I not only recognized, but honestly admired that his stomach wasn't the only one which growled.

Jack was insistent and unsatiated.

And he was reverent, even ravenous for life itself.

Lovely Up There

Impatient for information, Libby and I speak the day after our original call. She tells me that she's talked to Jack's sister, Avery, and has some news. She goes on to say that from what they've been able to piece together so far, Jack had hiked up into the mountains to White Ranch Park, a popular biking/hiking spot outside of Denver.

"It's lovely up there; the countryside is astounding," she says. "It's also where him and Susan got married."

We both wonder why that spot? A spiteful last jab? But this doesn't sound like the man I knew.

She tells me Jack bought the gun sometime in January.

More wonder. How long had he been planning this?

She tells me that he had been having a rough time. A hard spot in his life. That he had just gotten a small, one bedroom apartment, but never bothered to unpack or decorate. But even though he felt depressed, he was determined to bounce back.

Again, we wonder. No unpacking? How strange. But then, that would be like Jack. He typically never had much interest in those kinds of things. And a lot of people are depressed. Hell, most of America is struggling. But most of them are still alive.

After we wander through our mutual minds, an unsuccessful attempt at sorting out the puzzle, we agree to speak soon. Nothing left to say except, "You *will* be coming to the memorial, won't you?" she asks. "When it happens."

Hesitation. "Maybe."

"I wish you would. Will you give me a call when you've made up your mind? Just so I know what's going on."

And high above us, a hawk screeches as I see Jack tapping his finger on the steering wheel for what seems like minutes, his face bunching up in a contemplative scowl.

"Absolutely."

Now, he's laughing. A gleeful giggle barely in control as we play chess.

"Okay. Well, I have some errands to take care of. Let's not go too long."

"Not too long," I agree.

Click.

I see him as we're speeding down the highway.

Ever faster toward the sun.

Counting Cows

Dazed with the notion that perspective lurked somewhere ahead.

Somewhere past the long span of deserted road between Eden and Farson, but before the mountains and forests of Pinedale and Jackson. Somewhere under the quiet emptiness of the air, but above a prairie steeped in purity. Apart from the prickly sense of society's madness—the hurly burly tumult and the fuss of profit and pressure—in conjunction with its unharmonious propriety and ruthless exploitation of nature.

Not here. Here there were moments. And within them an exhibit of a daydreamed life. With context scrawled on a clean slate. Meaning on full display. A landscape of time and hope. There was possibility as we sped by the endless fence lines. The occasional pole-mounted lamp. A corral. A shed or barn. And cows who dotted the prairie.

We were counting them.

A game we played.

The cattle made us both think of steak with baked potato. Sour cream and chives. Maybe some beans. Jack's stomach rumbled, but his gaze roamed far ahead; the steering wheel of the Mustang gripped. "Hypothesis. Does being critical of society, but still lending a hand to all its faults and failures, make us hopelessly satisfied and content within an illusion?"

"Conclusion. Not if we're convinced otherwise," I answered with a grin.

"Question. Does that make us clones of consumption?"

"Answer. Better than clones *for* consumption."

We both looked at the cows, then at each other.

He went on. "Hypothesis. If we're convinced we're in control of our past, present, and future, does that make us unaware?"

"Conclusion. Only fate can tell us."

The cows didn't seem to care, not even bothering to look up from the grass.

"Question. How do you know if you're really alive?" I asked.

"Answer. A calm moment of being."

One cow looked up and sedately regarded the others.

"Hypothesis," he followed. "If you look to the west for a new start; if you look to the horizon for some sort of exquisite freedom and rich opportunity. A new life. If you discard life on the east coast, leaving it behind not only physically but emotionally, are you doomed to failure? Are you doomed to bring everything with you? All your fears, prejudices, doubts, pains, traumas, angers, and resentments? Disappointments and failures? Misfortunes and mistakes?"

I thought for a few moments. Never once had it entered my mind to contemplate what he said. My only thought had been that I wanted out of New England. That I wanted to go west, like him, and try something fresh. To be new.

The cows seemed content to be where they were. Or at least they looked to be.

"Conclusion. No. You bring with you only what you choose."

Jack frowned. I could tell this bothered him. I could see his mind as it teetered back and forth. A synaptic seesaw, not sure how to feel. "Okay, question. If your previous life has been forgotten in favor of a new start, how do you know you're in that space completely?"

"Answer. Because the past is no longer with you."

Another frown. "Hypothesis. What if that's just a glimmer in the hands of a buffoon? Or a jokester with a quirky, vague belief in something more beyond? What if age, and with it, the weight of the past, cultivates bankruptcy of the most violent form? What if it instills a loss of innocence, thereby making the world feel less free, and more isolated?"

It was now my turn to frown; at the same time mentally checking off another cow. A loner. Separated from the herd. Off by itself. Whether it wanted to be alone or not, I would never know.

"A conclusion with a question. Do you think you're cynical? That's thirty, my friend."

"Nah, man. I'm realistic," he replied with a straight face. "I just counted thirty-six."

We quietly mused on the fate of the cows.

And our own.

Circles in April

Introspective while sitting at the picnic table, I light a cigarette and pull my Army field jacket close around me. Like my father's from ages ago—the one I wore as a ten-year-old—mine is now worn and faded; smudged with time.

I look out at the cold, winter-bare trees, at the clusters of forest that cling to the slopes and blanket the horizon—oaks, maples, and birch. Conical cedars and the sprawled branches of junipers. Out beyond the meandering stretch of piled rock. The long asphalt footpath and the hills surrounding it. Over to the small regional airport which is uncontrolled with no tower, one runway, and a couple of hangars. The few designated walking trails cutting through tangled brambles with dead ends. And along the levee ending with a dam, the reservoir, and this picnic table. To this hometown levee. Reservoir in check and pooled.

This isn't the first time I've been here.

To remember. To sort out my mind.

Only this time, I'm not alone.

I look at Alder 'Dee' West and fondness swells in my heart. Fondness because I'm happy I reconnected with my old high school friend when I came full circle, home to New England in 2009. The result of an accidental link through Facebook.

After a few messages, we decided on dinner at a local Indian restaurant. Then we began to take long walks. And more dinners. More walks. And we eased into what I would call a real friendship. A friendship of acceptance without judgment, of honesty without hesitation, of genuine affection and an ease of comfort that comes with not only us getting older, but a sense of ataraxia within who we are as people and as adults.

Now, we play Folf. We joke about reruns of *CHiPs*, *Emergency!*, *Kojak*, and *The Love Boat*. We have family get-togethers. Dinners. His kids mow my lawn. We give each other gifts—a *Star Trek* bath towel, Grateful Dead socks, a Bob Ross painting, solar tiki torches—and talk about what matters to us.

We're old enough now, comfortable enough to be our bare selves without hesitation or embarrassment knowing that it's okay with the other. Right down to musing upon how small our bladders are beginning to feel in the middle of the night, and to wonder at how our bones are creaking more and more. To meditate on how our beards are grayer and whiter rather than dark. To percolate on whether it's important or not to grow old gracefully. That inevitable, stooping process that's begun to creep into both of us.

I look into his eyes, eyes that are watching me, waiting for me.

"I wish he had called me," I say with a grimace.

"I doubt very much anything would've changed how it went down," he responds. "Jack was always thick headed when he'd made up his mind about something."

"Fucking stubborn bastard." I pause. "It's funny. From what I know so far, he didn't feel needed or wanted. I guess because he felt abandoned by everyone. So, what does he do? He shoots himself, leaving his kids to grow up without a father. I'm sure they're gonna need him or want him. What kind of fucked up logic is that? Besides, if he was here right now, I'd tell him – guess what, *I* need you in my life. *I* want you in my life."

"I would tell him the same." Dee nods, as if confirming something to himself. "Jack always had a strange sense of logic. Most of our conversations were complex; even cryptic. If you didn't take them at face value, they were difficult to understand – to understand him. They often left very little clues as to what I always perceived as his real depth. And when the conversation would veer in that direction, he always became very awkward and went into what I call his weird grin space. He would just sit there with that grin; wooden like a mask. It was only when we would take walks, when we were hitching somewhere, that he would feel like he was loosening up and becoming more comfortable. Like a kind of calm would come over him being out somewhere, in the middle of nowhere, on the road, hoping for a ride. And if he was in control of the conversation, he would become downright serene. Loosened up. All the tension I felt in him dropped."

"I felt that too when we talked."

"It was almost as if when he was perceived as a master of something, something he had achieved on his own, he felt good. That he was proud of himself, almost silently beckoning you to pat him on the back. And it was only then that he always became more pliable to anything that could happen."

"You've known him about as long as I have."

"Since middle school. Did I ever tell you how we first met?"

I cock my head and think for a moment. "Now that you mention it, no."

"He was riding Mathilda, his bike, one day after school, on the sidewalk near where Store 24 used to be up at the university. You remember that?"

"Yeah. There was a record store next to it. And I also remember Mathilda."

"Right. University Records. Well, he was riding it and took a huge spill, I mean a bad one, arms and legs flying everywhere in circles, wheels tumbling up and over him. Nasty. And a couple of other kids stood there laughing at him, but I went over and helped him up."

"Jack was always kind of clumsy. But I never wanted to tell him that. I think he was sensitive to it."

"Tell me about it. But you know, he loved to wrestle."

"I don't remember that."

Dee leans back and grins. "Oh sure. And he used to get aggressive. Like pissed off aggressive. He'd take me on and after a while he'd be there all dirty and shaking all over, a really cold look in him."

The silence between us returns.

Then, I ask the question I've been wanting to. "So, you tell me. What do you think was going on in his head?"

"Hard to say. Jack always had a way of losing himself. I can't count all the times he would just talk and talk and talk, and end up going in circles, until I finally said to him, 'Enough already. None of what you're saying is making any sense, Jack.'"

I can't help but laugh. A fond laugh because Dee's right, and I had always felt it was one of Jack's more endearing traits.

"And he would always give me that baffled look, as if astounded I wasn't following along with him," he adds.

"I know. I remember it the same way. He was such a smart fucker but couldn't find his way out of his head. Everyone in that family is super intelligent."

"Maybe he couldn't find his way out of this one. No way to rationalize staying alive or finding a way to outwit his pain."

"Maybe."

We look at each other, then our gazes wander. We don't have the answers.

I turn back to Dee. "Are you okay?"

A firm nod. "I am. I think he's an asshole for what he did, but there's nothing we can do about it."

After a time, we walk back to our cars. The air's gotten colder under the dimming, pale blue sky, and the sun's beginning to set, somber and gloomy.

All is quiet. Still.

"I have to admit, Dee, I'm really fucking angry with him," I state firmly. The tone and volume of my words startle even me. Sharp and trembling; on the edge of nasty.

He nods, his own voice distant, lost in the air. "Me too." He looks ahead to the horizon. "Are you going out to Colorado for the memorial?" he abruptly asks.

"Libby asked me that too. I don't know. I don't know if I'm ready to face something like that."

I breathe in the biting air. Winter has yet to let go. The buds of leaves have yet to feel brave enough to sprout forth with fresh brightness; to bask in the warmth of vernal opportunity.

Some call it the doldrums.

Or the pregnant pause before the circle of a season.

Soggy Miracle

"You're going."

"I am?"

"Ayup. Trust me," Jack said as he gripped the steering wheel. "We're going to have a great time."

And for the next two hours, sheets of water flooded over the side windows of the car while the feeble wipers frantically tried to keep up. The impotent headlights barely caught a glimmer of the white lines.

"Besides which, I'm only back for a short time, and how often do we get to do this?"

"Not as often as Chris did," I reply. "How many did he go to?"

"No idea. But they're only playing three nights here, this being the last one. We have to go tonight."

"And they're not getting any younger."

"Nor are we. And Jerry's hair is even whiter than the last time we saw them."

"That was eons ago in high school."

He acknowledged this with a sharp jerk of his neck and we were silent for a few minutes as we sped down the highway. Trucking west through Long Island. He was lost in thought, the way he often was when he was behind the wheel. Those times seemed to bring out the meditative part of him. Some people think when they mow the lawn. Others in the bathroom, or when they cook. For Jack, the road was the place to contemplate life.

"So, interesting facts for the evening," he began. And I knew I was in for a good conversation. I sat up a little in my seat as he went on, "the Grateful Dead rose to become central hippies, what you might call the counterculture movement; the counterculture offering a promise of something better than the established system—"

"I think it's interesting how San Francisco became some sort of central meeting point," I interjected.

"In what way?"

"Because it was out west."

"Good point."

"Are you going to San Francisco," I began, then stopped short. My singing had never been the best. "But *you* landed in Denver," I finished with a grin.

"Close enough." His face bunched up into a scowl. In thought again, I could tell. "For me, I find it interesting that all those hippies hitchhiked out there for the promise of something liberating," he mused.

"Promises are hard to keep."

"Indeed, they are. And history seems to have clued us in on the fact that the promises of those days were harder to keep than they imagined. Certainly, in the sense of how what started off as a radical, dare I say, positive change in culture, ended up becoming co-opted."

"How so?" I asked.

He thought for a moment. I could tell he was reviewing what he wanted to say, to be as accurate and clear as possible. Jack was always careful with his language. Meticulous, so he could be complete and leave nothing in doubt.

"It became co-opted because what began as a pure movement to initiate change in established America, digressed into what they were originally speaking out against."

"In what way?"

"In the sense that, in the end, after all the talk of being different and living what Garcia called an uncluttered life, they've indulged just as much in capitalism as the generation they were criticizing. They've become what I would call merchandizing mercenaries. They were in it, of course, to play music and change the world, but what isn't recognized very often is that they were also in it for the money. As much as they may have changed society, they really didn't. I just find it ironic."

"I think that may hold true for the entire generation as well."

"Agreed. Although that's a blanket statement. So, you have to wonder, out of all the turmoil of those years, what *did* we really gain?"

"I'm not so sure, but they still have great music." I paused and ran my fingers through my shoulder length hair. "And there is a certain magic to their shows. Something special that no other band has been able to produce."

"And they did change America, in one way or another."

"I guess you have to give them credit for that," I told him.

"I do. And speaking of super cool music, there's the coliseum."

We slowed and surveyed the jammed lot. Then, we cruised and circled, floating around on the wet pavement until a distant wharf appeared and we found ourselves shipwrecked in a nosebleed spot. As we quickly walked toward the sparkling light of the coliseum, our jackets buttoned up, our shoulders huddled against the deluge, I couldn't help but feel enthralled with the spectacle around us.

RVs. Vans. Buses. Sports cars. Some with tarps strung between them—mutual, communal shelters. Plumes of smoke rose here and there, either from small Hibachis and barbeque grills, or grateful lungs. I pulled the hood of my jacket closer around my head.

We moved on, Jack leading the way.

Shakedown Street. An impromptu village of sorts. Throngs of glazed eyes milled through the vending area and picked over tie-dyes of every color imaginable. Also, tapestries, curtains, necklaces, bracelets, earrings, ponchos, and handmade mugs. John Lennon sunglasses, even after dark. Teriyaki beef sticks. Bowls of Quinoa. Muffins. Cookies. And peace pipes and bongs. Some glass. Some metal or wood. Long and short.

Of course, for tobacco use only.

Despite our hurried pace, I caught Jack eyeing the sandwiches.

An occasional passerby, with a side-eyed glance and a muttered, "Acid," "Shrooms," or "Dime bag." Soggy cardboard signs with ink smeared handwriting:

I NEED A MIRACLE

The Americana counterculture was alive and well, here and now, in the early 90s. A whole world onto itself. But there was time pressure. The evening had folded full into night. And the show was about to start.

We had to find tickets.

Our own miracle.

An hour passed. Our belief in hope faded. Our sense of helplessness grew. The rain chilled our very marrow. But chance took pity on us. On the verge of giving up, a savior emerged from the congregation and darkness. A hooded sweat jacket profiteer with dreadlocks and waterlogged corduroys.

But he only had one.

Without hesitation, Jack paid him and turned to me. "Go."

"W-what about y-you," I stammered through my frigid teeth.

He smiled, a smile of fondness and generosity. "I'll be fine." His head bobbed toward the vendors. "Think I'll see if I can score a bag, maybe some shrooms and a sandwich. Meet me at the car when the show's over."

"Are you sure?"

"Yes," he replied with a quick shove toward the Nassau Veteran's Memorial Coliseum.

In the direction of the pot smoke clouds, the dilated acid pupils, the wild cocaine energy, the flickering stage lights, the spinners, the tapers, the 'Jerry's a God' gatherings, and the Phil section. At the older generation and the new, all bunched together into one blissful writhing mass. Into the improvised magic, where the audience drove the music, and the music played the band. And through an elemental rite of passage both familiar and unfamiliar.

But also, where the personal demons of circumstance, living certain ways, and making certain choices are kept hidden. Locked away and lost in a thicket of pain. Unspoken, until often too late. Avoided in favor of believing the answers to the madness in the world will end up as nothing more than a charming cosmic joke.

Without another word, Jack disappeared into the mandal of the parking lot.

Two days later, he called me. He'd been laid up in bed with reruns of *Barney Miller* and *Happy Days*, was achy and had a fever. "Seriously, dude, that was one of the best times of my life," he said through his stuffy nose.

Boxes, Part One

Late April, before leaving for Colorado.

I'm in the basement rummaging through the boxes I've stored. Boxes of memories I haven't looked through in years. At the bottom of this one, I come across what I've been looking for—my photos of Jack.

With a sense of relief, I sink down on my old army box. That old, black tote issued before I left. The one I lugged around Iraq and is now filled with paraphernalia from the war. A Coca-Cola can in Arabic. A small, wooden, hand-carved camel I bought in Kuwait for my mother. A few photos of me in the desert—next to my five-ton truck. Or near the flightline at Camp Anaconda. And at Doha, Cedar, Virginia, a few others. An ashtray made from spare sheet metal. A bracelet tied from parachute cord. Uniforms and rank insignia. My aviation wings. Medals—the Army Commendation Medal, Army Achievement Medal, Good Conduct, and more.

My trusty Zippo.

Clink, schnick.

And, of course, the handwritten journals which were transcribed into my first book.

○

The top picture is of us standing on the top of a spectacular mountain pass. It's winter; maybe '96. Could be '97, in Montana somewhere. I remember Rita, my ex-wife, took it. Clinging to each other, we're cold, and Jack's clutching his Greek fishing hat to his head because of the wind.

○

The second one's a little older. We're sitting on the floor of the apartment; the garden level apartment on Lafayette Street. I'm lying on my side looking up at Jack, who is sitting cross-legged, a bottle of Rolling Rock in front of his bare feet on the cheap, tan carpet. We're talking about our next road trip.

○

Another one from Colorado. A five-by-seven taken outside of the city. Deep in the mountains. Jack's standing on a summit. Which peak? I don't recall now. His backpack is leaning against his leg. A proud, happy frontiersman. Behind him is a breathtaking view of the Rockies. The world from 13,000 feet.

○

Here's a smiling Jack in Utah, somewhere around Bryce Canyon. We're about to hike a gorge, a chasm of gorgeous red/orange rock.

○

In this one, he's resting his ass on my old red Honda Civic in Idaho, hands tucked in the front pockets of his jeans. The sleeves of Jack's white, long underwear shirt are rolled up. It's winter, and we're out in the middle of nowhere. Somewhere. Some tiny, one-gas-station town. I can't remember the year.

○

A four-by-eight snapshot in Utah near the Nevada border. I think we were on our way to Great Basin National Park. Taken by me from the Mustang's passenger seat, Jack's standing on the side of the road with an amused state trooper. Posed, they're looking directly into the camera as the trooper is handing Jack a speeding ticket. The trooper was shocked at first when we asked if we could take a picture of his souvenir from the state. But he'd been a great guy, and he had quickly agreed.

○

The next we're at my wedding in Montana. In a dark gray suit, Jack is best man. He's standing in front of Rita, extending a wine glass, and toasting the happy, new couple. That was May of 2000.

○

Underneath that one is a polaroid of the two of us kneeling under a tinseled Christmas tree with colored lights. Arms wrapping around each other, my left hand is holding a plastic, toy lightsaber. I spot my mother's handwriting across the top of the picture:

Dana and Jack 1977

○

One year further back. The earliest one. Small fingers clutching plastic forks while eating birthday cake with my father at the kitchen table. Even he looks happy.

○

Cub Scouts. We're marching in a parade, but I can't remember which one. Dark blue uniforms complete with full sets of badges—Tiger, Wolf, Bear, and Webelos. Gold and silver arrowheads. Patches on our shoulders—Den 56 and the American flag. Beaded diamonds—Progress Toward Ranks—are hanging from the buttons of the front pockets.

○

At the bottom of the pile are two photographs of us at the beach. A portrait of a gray, cloudy day at Rocky Neck State Park in Niantic, Connecticut. We're probably about twelve years old and standing with my mother, her arms around our shoulders. My panting dogs, tongues lolling out of their mouths, are sitting in front of all of us. An accompanying landscape shows these two best friends kneeling and gathering seashells on the beach.

○

In all of these photos, we're smiling.

Everyone.

Then my chest tightens with something near to sadness as it occurs to me.

I'm the only one left alive.

Nazi

"My mom says my grandfather was killed because of people like you," the boy with the blonde hair yelled.

I was scared, shocked, frozen in time. I didn't know what to do. I also didn't understand.

Jack didn't look different. Didn't talk different. Didn't walk different. Didn't smell different. Didn't weigh different. His hair wasn't combed differently. His skin color wasn't different. His arms and his legs, eyes, nose, and ears weren't different. He had the same schoolbooks. Wore the same clothes. Took the same bus. Ate the same lunches. Played the same games at recess. And he got in trouble for a passed note.

Jack was like everyone else.

"Is your Dad Hitler?" accused one of the boys.

"Yeah, he is," admonished another. "And you're a Nazi."

As was so often the case when I was a child and into my young adult years, my voice failed me. Muted, before the war both forced and enlightened me through life threatening situations to overcome the silence of my tongue. I wanted to shrink away. Hide into myself. Shy away from confrontation, all while telling myself that it was the better, higher road to let bullies be bullies and not dignify them with fighting back. My stomach quivered and my face was flush.

I wanted to run.

But Jack stood defiantly before them with his lips tightened in mute defense, his arms crossed in front of him. His eyes met theirs, both steady and calm, until he spoke. "If you knew anything, you would know that the time of the Nazi party is over, assholes." Then, he turned to me. "Come on, Dana. Let's go. They're not worth shit."

"Look, he's walking away. Must be a sissy Nazi," chided the first boy.

"Nazi," squawked one of them.

"Nazi," whooped another.

"Nazi...Nazi...Nazi...Nazi," chorused all three of them.

As we listened to the boy's chant fade around the bend of his road I asked, "What did they mean by all that?"

"It's because I'm German, and Carl teaches it up on campus," his shaky voice muttered as he squeezed his eyes shut to subdue his tears.

I looked at my best friend with admiration. Admiration because he stood up to them. He already knew what I didn't. That Nazis, war, bullies, all our intolerances, fears, and prejudices live only in the hearts of those who first imagine them.

Admiration turned to shame. If I had had the courage and the knowledge, maybe my voice wouldn't have failed me.

Maybe I wouldn't have failed him.

You're Gonna Miss Me

"I just feel, with new scenery, I can get more of a sense of who I want to be without all these infernal ghosts hovering over my shoulders," he affirmed as he swept his arms around in a broad circle to his house, the woods. What I assumed was our town and surrounding state. He tossed a forest green duffel over the rusted back fender and into the back of his midnight-blue metallic Ford F-150. The truck with the rear bumper that clung to the frame with zip ties and duct tape.

"It's a long way to Colorado, Jack. Are you sure?"

He leaned his arm on the side of the bed, looked at me, and smiled. "I'm going the way of the pioneers, tippin' my hat back and grabbin' the reins." The smile turned into a broad grin. "Only with a pickup. You're gonna miss me."

A statement, not a question.

I looked down at the ground and toed a chunk of gravel from the driveway; the driveway of his childhood home. "Yeah." I looked up. "Yeah, I am."

"Well, you don't have to. Why don't you come with me?"

"I can't."

"Why not?"

"Well…"

"Balderdash. You could go pack a bag and jump in this afternoon if you wanted to."

"Like you?"

"Not so much like me. I've been planning this for about two years now. Ever since my Dad and my brother."

"You never told me about it."

It was his turn to toe the gravel. "No need to."

"But it's so soon after graduation. I mean, it's only been three weeks since high school got out. What's the rush? We have plenty of time. Don't you want to hang out for a little while? Spend the summer kickin' around the ol' stomping grounds?"

He looked up with that serious gaze from his blue/gray eyes. "Nope." He reached out and squeezed my shoulder. "It's time, Dana. I have to go."

Love & Patience

'I am so sorry that I haven't been in touch more. This period in my life is turning out to be an incredible growth experience for me and is turning out to create so much more self-knowledge and insight into my true self. It's really crazy and eye-opening. I look forward to reconnecting with you and having you in my life again. Thank you so much for reaching out to me and for the love and patience that you have shown always for me as my path takes me to so many isolated places that make it very hard to connect with me. This lonely marriage and therapy are making me realize very much how much deep and healthy connection I want and need in my life. I am so grateful to you that you have always been a part of my life, who found a way to connect with me in my different places and phases. I love you very much my brother.'

I'm staring at Facebook. At a final instant message sent not more than a month ago. And I'm so very melancholy with the knowledge that I wasn't there for him. With him. And somewhat indignant. Indignant with an almost desperate wish that he would've let me. But deep down, I know my friend all too well. I know he never would've let me.

Nothing left to do but get on the road.

Substance

Lost in thought, I'm driving with the window rolled down, my arm over the side of the door, dangling in the wind.

Being on the road is different this time. But I don't know how. I only know it's fitting that after all the time Jack and I spent in cars, I don't fly. Taking a plane feels like an affront. A flimflam expedition without substance, as if I'm trivializing our experience, exploration, and adventure.

Our friendship.

'Have I made the right decision? What can I possibly achieve by driving all this way?'

'Dude, you know that a road trip is not so much about the destination as it is about the journey,' says Jack from the empty passenger seat.

I nod. *'Hi Jack.'*

'Hello back. Hope you don't mind me coming along for the ride.'

'Of course not. That's the way it's always been. Wouldn't have it any other way.'

Out of all the times I've crisscrossed the country, this trip feels the most surreal. Displaced somehow. Fidgety and dizzy with a sense that my foot isn't really on the accelerator. Eyes not on the highway with my heart lost somewhere in a hallucination of despondency.

This can't be happening. And going to Colorado won't change

a damn thing. It won't change the memories I have and won't change time.

Or certainty.

Or truth.

Only Superman can make the world spin backward.

A Mystical Pinch

Three years after we graduated from high school, Jack had long since moved to Denver. We had wanted to see each other, and travel for a while, so I was on my way. Conveniently, he landed in LaGuardia Airport because of his new job as a flight attendant, although I can't remember which airline now.

Because he had a few days off until his schedule picked up, we thought it would be fun to drive to Denver together. To maximize our time out west, we decided to take shifts driving; to go all the way nonstop except for gas, bathroom, and food breaks. Coffee, the Grateful Dead, conversation, and of course, Jack's curious affinity toward convenience store sandwiches, would keep us fueled.

I drove first.

Just outside of New York, he shifted uncomfortably, then took a deep breath.

"What's up?" I asked.

"My leg's been bothering me. It's the long hours serving cans of Coke to the passengers," He exhaled. "And all the walking through airports."

"Even after all this time? It's been a few years now."

"It's something I'll probably have to live with for the rest of my life."

I glanced at him out of the corner of my eye. The change in his demeanor was readily apparent from when I picked him up. At first, he'd looked alert and bright as he slung his suitcase—one of those efficient, wheeled ones used by frequent travelers—onto the back seat, opened the passenger door, and got into my beat-up, fire engine red '89 Honda Civic. He'd looked sharp with a sense of confidence; a debonair pilgrim seeing the world with his clean shaven face and medium brown hair cut short. A professional dressed in navy blue trousers and vest, not his usual jeans and T-shirt. Golden, shiny wings. A nameplate, tie, and a light blue button up dress shirt that neatly hid his shoulder tattoo of the Tasmanian Devil—a caption wrapped around it:

A Friend of the Devil is a Friend of Mine

But now, he looked contemplative. Serious. A furrow digging into his brow.

"Whatcha thinkin'?" I asked.

"I'm glad New England and New York are behind us. I always feel better when we're headed west."

Startled by his grave tone, I turned to him. "Why?"

"It's too closed in. Claustrophobic. I feel like I'm buried somehow. Besides which, you can't see a lot of sky with all the hills and trees."

I could empathize. Like him, I too had felt stifled during our childhood, those years in New England as I longed to explore new places, my imagination a constant companion. But the weight he seemed to feel wasn't as heavy for me. And I had thought that moving to Denver might alleviate some of that load. That he might have somehow felt more illuminated, more buoyant, and less weighed down during a visit. Apparently, he didn't. And that made me curious. Were the ghosts he'd told me of three years ago still bothering him? I decided to keep our conversation lighthearted.

I chuckled. "Well, foliage season is nice."

He looked at me for a minute or so. Penetrated me. It made me slightly uncomfortable. "True. You have me there. And at least the humidity is more bearable in autumn. But I've always found it to be oppressive and intolerable in more ways than just during the summer."

"So, you like the west because it's more open?"

"Absolutely. And dry. I feel free and clean; not greasy. Besides, New England doesn't really have a lot to offer. There's no National Parks to speak of, only Acadia up in Maine, and no open wilderness. Nothing to do but bore yourself to death."

"How spiritual," I replied dryly.

"Not really. More of a mystical pinch in the ass reminding me to be original and to leave shitty ol' New England in the rearview mirror. Besides, there's a certain seduction about stepping on the gas pedal."

"I hear ya there."

He sighed again. "Fuck it. Let's put on some Dead. That, at least, my psyche welcomes without permission."

From my meager tape collection that rested in the center console, he plucked out *Workingman's Dead* and fast-forwarded a few tracks without bothering to look at the song list. The lament of the ill-fated Casey Jones began to thrum from the speakers.

'Trouble ahead

Trouble behind...'

He leaned back in the seat and closed his eyes, then murmured, "My brother always liked this tune."

"Yeah, I remember him playing it when we were in high school."

"That and Bear's Choice. He wore that album out."

"I know."

"Did you also know that this song bears some resemblance to the original Casey Jones it's supposed to be about? The real Casey Jones was an American railroad conductor in the late 1800s and being someone who preferred to be punctual, he was speeding one night because he was late. When he got to the station down in Mississippi, there was another train in his way, and he was killed when he averted crashing into it. I think it's cool that he saved everyone on that train, but himself."

"No shit?"

"No shit. And he even got the train there on time."

Dark clouds peeked through the dense canopy of trees along the highway, as Scranton, Pennsylvania (home of the Houdini Museum) came into view.

Together, along with five sandwiches, seven iced teas, and roughly forty Grateful Dead songs playing over and over, we made Denver in thirty-eight hours.

Lafayette Street

In the living room sitting cross-legged on my black, plastic milk crate, I watched the last rays of golden light dissipate from the two, small, rectangular basement windows set into the concrete wall.

Across from me and our dining table/workout bench, was Jack, squatted on his own milk crate. A rectangular Styrofoam takeout container rested on his knees as a plastic fork vigorously scooped up piles of Japanese. The hottest beef curry he could find at the Ikano Bowl; so hot that beads of sweat broke out on his forehead and dampened his fine, brown hair.

Terrapin Station played through the stereo system he had set up. The tidal melody submerged the twenty-four-hour drone of downtown. Four speakers, each in a corner. Tall piles of CDs haphazardly gathered around the receiver which sat along one wall, on the cheap, tan carpet. A few weights for his morning routine. And an aged Chess board, the pieces ready to be moved.

The rest of the room was bare.

One poster of The New Metropolitan Museum of Art – The American Wing was tacked to the wall. The only decoration. Ever the curious intellectual, it symbolized not only his personality—depth, art, and acumen—but what he found irrelevant and quarrelsome to his life—materialism, triviality, and ignorance.

Three other small rooms made up the rest of our garden level paradise—a kitchen, a bathroom, and a bedroom.

The kitchen floor was old with broken white porcelain tiles. A butter colored 1970s compact stove with an analog clock/timer filled one wall. The half-sized refrigerator along the other was even older. A miniscule sink, older still. And a counter only large enough to fit a plastic dish rack. On it was a saucepan, an old, white ceramic coffee mug and a few plastic cups.

The phone booth bathroom had a shower—a quarter circle with a blue and white tile perimeter—next to a stand-alone sink. A stained, cloudy mirror, smudged from years of chronic moisture, hung crooked above it. A towel was slung over the top edge of the door.

Our shared bedroom contained his single mattress which sagged on a bare metal frame. I had the concrete floor with my sleeping bag, my clothes piled next to it. Both of us enjoyed an overhead landscape of the lacy cracks threaded through the walls where the pipes and heating ducts hung.

All the rooms were cramped, even without humans. But we didn't mind. In '95, in our early twenties, it was home.

A cozy lodging under Denver.

And we even spent an evening smoking pot and sticking glow-in-the-dark constellations to the ceiling of the bedroom. Two hundred thirty-three fragments of sky; our own sky. With a big full moon and comets and planets. I liked putting up Saturn. He liked setting the moon. At night, we lounged in our respective corners, talked into the wee hours, and gazed at the universe above. According to Jack, I didn't get the position of The Big Dipper right.

We were young, fresh and alive with springtide buoyancy. The years didn't have weight, and anything was possible. Full of energy and ready to chase down our whims. Bar hopping, smoking pot behind a club (sometimes with a bouncer), waiting in the Drive Thru lane at two-thirty in the morning for a Taco Bell burrito knowing we were getting up in a few hours for work. It all seemed the way it was supposed to be.

There was time.

Bouncing back was not a problem. A quick rub of eyes, a shower, and a tall cup of java was all that was needed. And we were always ready to do it the next night. And the next. Maybe even the one after that. If there was a job, the meager income we earned was enough for rent and bills, booze and weed. And a little leftover for food and gas. That was all we needed.

"So, how long do you think it will take the city to fix the pipes?" I inquired.

His fork stirred the curry as he turned and looked through the windows, then back at me. "Well, considering the whole backyard is a mountain of mush, I don't know. It could be a while."

I speared a dumpling and ate it in one bite. "At least they left us a path to the door."

"Considerate of them, wasn't it?"

I smiled. "I'm just glad it'll be fixed. Showering with raw sewage around my ankles this morning really sucked."

"Yeah, I bet it did. Not a pretty picture, to say the least."

"Well, you know, I like to live like a rock star."

Scooping and shoveling the last bits of his curry into his mouth, he got up and headed into the kitchen. From over his shoulder I heard, "We aim to please. Nothing but first-class accommodations."

I chuckled, ate another dumpling, then shifted on my crate.

A moment later, his voice filtered through the concrete wall. "Oh, dude."

"What?"

"The ants are crawling up the walls again."

I got up and went to see, carrying my dinner with me and lancing another dumpling on the way. Around the corner, I saw a long trail of ants. A black army of soldiers, one after another, from the sink to the ceiling. We stood there for a moment, each of us fascinated with how purposeful and enterprising they were.

Then he turned to me. "You wanna go on a road trip?"

Buffalo Balls

Hot breath blasted my arm; my face.

Humph.

"Don't move," he said flatly.

The flame of my Bic went out, the cigarette hanging limply from my lips as I slowly turned toward the open window. There, before me in all its majestic magnificence, loomed the matted, furry head of a buffalo. One perfectly round chocolate brown eye the size of a half dollar gazed at me with keen alertness and bland curiosity.

Humph.

This time its breath fanned my face as the eye took in what the buffalo might've thought were something like rabbits caught in a hole. Small creatures to nudge with its wet nostril which flared as it took in our scent. A long, sinuous thread of snot oozed from its snout above my arm.

Plop.

"How ridiculous," Jack said with a grin.

Then, slow, lazily, the nose inched further into the Mustang. Obviously, not at all threatened.

"Holy shit," exclaimed Jack. "Just its nose fits into the car."

"Umm," was all I could manage.

"Smells like a moose's ass," he muttered with a grimace.

With a languorous sweep of its head, the buffalo withdrew from the cabin. After a farewell grunt, he moseyed around toward the front end of the car.

Clomp, clomp, clomp, clomp.

Jack put the Mustang into Park and shut off the engine.

At two-thousand-pounds and six feet in height, the behemoth took up semi-permanent residence for a long, unhurried panoramic view of his surroundings—the quiet meadow grass and the serene pines scattered in with the firs. The quarter mile herd of sightseers who gawked and chattered from the edge of the pavement.

There he stood; a full-grown bison.

A bison who towered over our car, unconcerned with the Mustang and the inhabitants who trembled within. He swiveled his enormous head left, then right. As he dillydallied on his proverbial "red carpet," I fancied that I could see a grin on his face as he posed for the paparazzi's holiday home video documentaries and scrapbook exposés.

"You have to admire the size of those balls," asserted Jack.

"Umm…impressive," was all I could manage again.

A high-pitched shriek from across the road startled us, making us jump in our seats. In conjunction, we turned our heads and peered into the jam of RVs parked along the shoulder. Into the throng of striped Polos, khaki chinos, and leather loafers. Flowery summer dresses and strappy sandals. Greasy hamburgers and hot dogs. A melting fudgesicle.

"Oh my God, don't *hit* it," screamed a middle-aged woman who clutched a super-sized bucket of popcorn.

Jack looked at me.

I looked at Jack.

A few moments passed.

But because no words were needed to communicate how ludicrous this notion was, we helplessly burst into rolls of hysterical laughter.

The Heart of It All

Cruising west through Pennsylvania, I know now one thing that's changed; what's different about being on the road. My suspicion being that there's more I'm going to discover.

I used to intentionally crack just about every bone in my body—knees, toes, neck, back, knuckles, and wrists. Now, they crunch on their own. And I have temple gray. I can't cruise in the driver's seat as long as I used to because of aches. That and my bladder needs emptying more often and my bowels don't like to move. I don't bounce back as fast, even after I rest. The bottom line is that the liabilities which fall with the autumn of life are upon me.

Plus, I no longer feel the magic of the road. I don't marvel at the world as I once did. No original wonder. I feel no urge to broaden my mind through travel because besides my physical aging, the war stole my enthusiasm for new experiences. My mind and my eyes steeped in cynical realism. So, while I still love the idea of road tripping, the actuality of them is far less frequent, as I'm edgy about leaving the sanctity of home.

The bottom line is I've often felt that the war took ten years off me. In a way beyond the convictive use of language. And the tension of consideration nags me. The weariness of consequence scolds me. The guilt of age pulls me.

But amid the violence and death, and the loneliness, I did have

Jack. His relentless support and encouragement through emails, letters, and care packages were largely what gave me hope and carried me through those plodding days. He kept my soul from completely withering. Helped salvage the remains.

'Dude, I couldn't let you do that alone,' says Jack from the empty passenger seat.

'I never told you, Jack, but your love was one of the things that saved my life.' I pause. *'Why didn't you let me do the same?'*

No answer as I pass through the border into Ohio.

Welcome to

THE HEART OF IT ALL

Our Kids

"Welp, we have to go through this in order to find our way home," Jack informed me. "It's the shortest way, and the only way with a reward at the end – unless you want to go back the way we came, which is never a good idea. Should we go for it?"

"Fuck, yeah. It would be a total embarrassment to go back to Denver with a clean truck."

"You're right."

We were stopped in the middle of a dirt road, far up in the mountains, on a gorgeous, dry, warm day. A few cotton ball clouds hung in the azure sky. Lodgepole pines, junipers, aspens, spruce, and firs as far as we could see. They clustered over the slopes, the ridges and summits, the saddles, the notches and draws. We had spent the afternoon carefree, exploring every rocky track we could find in his Toyota 4Runner—one of three he owned; the other two being organ donors.

The air was still except for the purr of the idled engine.

We gazed at the thin, snaky wagon trail ahead, and at the muddy puddle (rain from the night before) that took up half of it. A good twenty feet anyway.

"You ready?"

"Yep. I mean we *are* the kings of soggy four-wheeling, after all."

"Aficionados of buggyin'."

"Connoisseurs of the Colorado Car Wash."

"That's us."

Mutual grins.

We rolled up the windows. The windshield wipers came to life. He gunned the engine, and it growled with ecstasy. I grabbed onto what we fondly called the 'Oh My God Bar' above the passenger window. At about twenty-five miles per hour, we hit it. The hood dipped as brown slop splashed up and over the windshield, over the roof, and along the side. We couldn't see for a second. Then the hood rose up above the sightline of the road. The cab wobbled, rocked, and shook us back and forth in our seats.

"Whoo-hoo," I yelled.

Thuuu…wunk.

With a lurch forward that activated our seat belts, we stopped.

The truck was at an angle of about fifteen degrees, with the front tires on the lip of the puddle. They spun helplessly, along with the back ones. Jack rolled down his window, turned, looked back, then turned to me. "Shit, man, we're stuck."

We stared at each other for a few moments, the shock to our overblown, counterfeit four-wheel egos overwhelmed, then burst into laughter.

"Try not to get water in here when you get out, okay?" he said, as he opened his door.

We got out, calf deep water seeping into our socks and shoes, and soiling our jeans. We sloshed to the back of the truck like soldiers through a swampy tropical marsh.

"Wow, we really buried those wheels, didn't we?" I exclaimed, almost breathless with awe at our triumphant accomplishment.

"Yep," is all he could say while he scratched his head. A dry frown stretched across his face. "Let's take a look along the side of the road for some timber, rocks – anything we can find to put under them to give us some traction."

"Cool."

We worked together, positioned nature's tools, rocked the truck back and forth, and about forty-five minutes later, we managed to release it from its aqueous confines. Safe on the other side of the puddle, now smeared from head to toe, we climbed into the truck. And as the sun set behind us, we wound our way back to Denver.

"You know, we were way out of our depth. We probably should've checked the puddle first," I concluded.

"We've been way out of our depth for a long time, probably since long before we can remember. But you're right, that would've been a good idea. Think of it this way. Someday, it'll be something to tell our kids about. Something our parents never did as they frittered away in the suburbs while fucking us up."

The Whole Shooting Match

We were in a restaurant somewhere on Long Island. Originally a large colonial house, but now with freshly painted fire engine-red wood siding. New, double paned, white trimmed double-hung windows. And a large sign planted in the front yard with two sturdy posts, surrounded by tidy, well-trimmed shrubs—Rhododendrons, most of them long past their radiant blooming, their once bright green leaves turning to bronzy red and beginning to drop for the coming winter.

A creamy scent of butter hung in the air. The damp cling of light steam billowed from the kitchen. The soft clatter of dinner conversation caressed our ears, interrupted now and then by the crack of a lobster claw. We acknowledged the final gesture of good will from a server, "Would you like a slice of lemon in your water?"

A cool autumn evening when heaters are just being turned on.

We sat at a short, raised platform with a railing that enclosed our table and one other from the rest of the eatery. Our table was small, square, and covered by glass, a red and white checkered tablecloth underneath it. On the wall next to us was a photo of a sailing ship surrounded by icebergs of all sizes and shapes, enclosed by a scratched, bare wood frame. A black and white print of a lone outpost of survival on an otherwise barren, immense, and frigid sea.

The ship looked isolated, yet resilient. Proud, yet unsure. Strong, yet pinched from the ice. A small, brass plaque with an etching was tacked to the bottom of the frame:

HMS ENDURANCE 1915

I could almost hear Ernest Shackleton yelling, "She's going boys. It's time to get off."

Jack had ordered the lemon garlic shrimp linguini. When it arrived, he instantly began to devour massive rolls of pasta topped with a shrimp on his fork. It was as if he was untrusting of when the ocean would pour in through buckled wooden planks.

As my fork hovered above my plate of baked salmon over rice with asparagus, I couldn't help but watch with astonishment. As my mouth hung open with silent perplexity.

I forked an asparagus spear and asked, "Dude, don't you want to take the shells off?"

Jack shrugged. "Nah. Eating this way, the way I do, I get the full monty..." He began to chew and crunch his way through a bite. "...the contrast of hard and soft, the bitter and the sweet..." More crunch, more chew. "...because life is about the whole shooting match and nothing less," he ended with a grin.

Interlude, Part One – The Mulberry Sky

Being a workaholic, my father was deeply displaced when, in 2016, he was fired from his part-time retirement job. Right or wrong, the justification was age, because according to his superior's not-so-subtle tones, he had outlived his usefulness. As a result, because his very identity and sense of individuality was lost, he became terrified. And despite having everything in the material sense, a profound depression soon followed.

To make things worse, the quintessential, model family life—which he had desperately willed into existence—had deteriorated to the point of silence with my mother, a woman pillaged from her alcoholism and their ongoing conflict—a fifty-year, give or take, war of the roses. And her sheer hatred of him and his resentment toward her provided the awful sensation that he had never been appreciated or supported or validated. Needed or loved. I can't recall a single kiss or an anniversary celebration.

I didn't help.

Two months into his depression, he visited me with, at the time it seemed, a simple attempt to say hello. But so consumed with the publication of my first book, and how he had ignored my own attempts at communication, I angrily told him I was busy and that he would have to wait until I was free.

I never got back to him.

So, with all this heaped on his shoulders—his unwillingness to embrace a new perspective, the torment of the past, and his sense of failure—one fine summer day his depression gave way to an irresistible impulse to simply give up.

An emotional pink slip.

A past due invoice with every mistake, misfortune, and consequence listed.

Early one morning, he wrote a short note and rested it carefully on his bedroom dresser. Then he slipped into the kitchen, took a chef's knife from the wooden holder, and silently—as he had done for so many years while employed—left the house. A house on a winding road on the top of a low hill. The house where I grew up, and where he busied himself with the lawn, raking the leaves, and clearing the driveway of snow. Where he devoted himself to the construction of a new pantry for my mother, stained the decks, and painted the roof soffits. Where he threw tennis balls for the dogs. Where, in the basement, he watched *Stripes* with Jack and me. Where he ate birthday cake with us. And where he had overseen sleepovers and backyard campouts.

The same house where, four years later, I received the call about Jack's suicide.

Defeated and unrushed, my father strode past the neatly placed trash and recycle bins by the side of the driveway. Past the tall, bushy Rhododendron out front—the one with the big, ruffled white blooms and little stalks capped in yellow. The one he planted, fertilized, and trimmed for years. And then into the oaks, birch, and hemlock trees. After about two hundred yards—past the charred remains of the forest fire and near the swamp—he found an old oak with a beautiful canopy of leaves and made himself comfortable.

I don't know how long he sat there, lost in the stillness of the forest, listening to the birds chirp and the squirrels crack open acorns. As the breeze brushed the foliage, and the clouds passed overhead. As the bright day began to wane, and the first star peeked from the Mulberry sky. Before my father aimed for his heart and pushed the knife between his ribs.

Not once. Not twice. But three times.

He missed. And that was the sole reason he lived (so I was told by the surgeon at the hospital) until I, along with a state trooper, found him six hours later, oblivious, and nearly dead, in a pond of blood which had soaked into last year's bed of leaves.

Two years later, while eating dinner—after the death of my mother and I had taken the role of caregiver—he unexpectedly shared that day with me.

He told me that a sensation of calmness flooded through him as he looked down at the knife cradled in the palm of his hand; as he watched two bumblebees stuck in his blood, their little legs leaving small, swirly trails. He said that he was filled with a harmonious quiet which compelled him to let go of everything. Placid, he had no past, present, or future. And the depth of his pain dissipated. He felt entirely, finally, accepted, forgiven, and loved. Peaceful with the buoyant understanding that a better place awaited.

Then, he smiled and continued eating his meatloaf, mashed potato, and broccoli. I nodded silently and continued to wash some dishes, too uneasy with my guilt to inquire more.

The clearest memory I have of my father's suicide attempt is just before the paramedics rushed him to the hospital. Strapped to the wheeled gurney, drenched in his blood, he looked at me as I stood nearby while the ambulance doors began to close. Into the empty air, he reached out a hand, his eyes full of anguish.

"I'm sorry, Dana," he whispered.

I nodded, too filled with sorrow to talk or cry.

For my father—as with many men—trauma from the past, unfulfilled, superficial relationships, fear of rejection, inadequacy, unimaginative convention, the impulse for overinvestment in work, and the suburban home ideal suffocate identity resilience.

Jack bought a gun.

I put a barrel in my mouth.

Carl took a bottle of pills.

My father stabbed himself.

But we all have our own ways of committing suicide before we die.

Heroes on Black Ice

Past midnight and cold as he gazed out at the dark night of Indiana.

"To be clear," meditated Jack from the passenger seat as he munched on a gas station chicken salad sandwich, "a lot of language and life can be viewed as metaphor."

I leaned back in the driver's seat and smiled, ready for another conversation. For another philosophical rant which stimulated me and challenged my mind. And this one more so. This one intrigued me because I reveled in playing with words. I liked toying with notions of how reality compared with its phrasing. One of numerous places where I tended to get lost in anything I read.

"This hope of shedding the past and starting a new life by going west," he continued, "has to do with a mythology of the mind, the heart, and the soul. It's a conviction that one can shape a new microcosm within the macrocosm of a new place. That because of the physical location, something will be different."

I nodded.

We'd covered this ground before, but I could tell it wasn't settled for him yet. I was curious to find out where he would take it this time. "Sure, I can see that. I think there's a certain born-again feeling that comes from a fresh beginning. Do you believe it?"

He took another bite of his sandwich and nodded. "I do. I do because you see the cars of others who get off their own highway—"

"Off an exit to nowhere," I interrupted with a grin.

"Right. Resigned to be stuck where they are."

"You gotta feel badly for them, but you pass their exit."

"No doubt. Clearly, they're baffled because life's on hold for them until they can get back on the road."

"Yeah, yeah, yeah. They haven't arrived at where they should."

"Or wherever they've been told to go."

I was thoroughly engaged now; elated even, with the enjoyment of the words. But also because I knew with conviction then that Jack and I were different. That night we were wrapped in the stubborn bubble of our dreams. Our imagination we were determined to actualize. With pasts outrun, we were plowing forward into the future with a smug, self-righteous feeling that others couldn't. A glimpse of an inkling that we were doing it, while they weren't. And everything was safe to form within the shelter of our car.

Whatever it was. Whoever they were.

It didn't matter.

"We're not afraid. Nothing's holding us back. We're still in the race. Still driving. Still moving forward," I countered.

I stepped on the gas and the speedometer hit seventy-five.

Jack finished his sandwich.

"I like to think that we're similar to the trees in Kansas or Nebraska, South Dakota or Wyoming," he declared. "Or here, on I-70. We're alone but still standing tall. The roots of our singularities have dug in deep. We've withstood all the elements that have been thrown at us over the years. All that cold snow of doubt, the blistering sun of hesitancy, and the pelting rain of scorn."

"Dude, that's awesome. Great wording. How about resilient? Tenacious? Impervious?"

Jack smiled. "All great words too." He paused, his smile fading, his words dropping to a whisper. "We're better now; now that we've left."

"And we're steadfast and distinct—"

"Now that we're free," he said, finishing my sentence.

"But are you happy?" I asked. "Now that you've arrived."

He shrugged. "I don't know. I guess I'm merely wondering why I still feel uneasy."

I shrugged too. "I honestly couldn't say, Jack."

"I think it's because conviction is fragile. Tenuous. It's slick and precariously balanced on the assumption that as long as your tires are spinning and gripping the road, then the present and the future will never cause you to slip."

Up ahead, I spotted a car stopped on the shoulder.

"Anyway—" he continued.

"Hey look," I interrupted.

He looked over his shoulder, then turned to me. "Hmm. How odd."

"Probably getting some rest for the night."

"Or fucking."

I chuckled.

A mile down the highway. Another car. Another mile. Another car. And another. And another. And another. One faced the wrong way.

"Maybe we ought to stop," he suggested.

"Okay."

Seventy-five miles per hour slowed to zero. Gear lever put in Park; the doors were opened, frigid outside air rushing in, rudely pushing away the warmth of our cozy microcosm. Our physical and philosophical refuge from the darkness.

We climbed out.

Two pairs of sneakers flailed and floundered. And two twenty something asses slapped the black iced pavement. With wide eyeballs staring, four hands scrambled up and clung to the side rails of the roof.

"Holy shit," I gasped.

He laughed. "I think that's a reminder that we shouldn't feel too much like entitled heroes."

God, Sex, Guns, & Chocolate

A billboard on the side of the highway:

You Can Talk to God like Jesus Did.
Just Join Us.

'Naturally, a father and son can always speak to one another,' says Jack from the empty passenger seat.

Ohio summer heat. Indiana humidity. Illinois sticky. Missouri sweaty.

My 'Steal Your Face' T-shirt bunching up against the seat.

Another billboard:

Matrimony is one man and one woman...only

'I guess variety isn't the spice of life after all,' I state through a grin.

The Midwest; home of the swing states. Also the states that decide national elections.

The people who are lovers of curds, pop, coney dogs, and puppy chow; don't forget the Ranch dressing. They live amid rich green fields dotted with hickory, oak, walnut trees, and the occasional funky whiff of manure. Among silos, tractors, barns. All in seas of corn, grain, soybeans, and wheat. And they're some of the friendliest folks around. If you happen to share their values.

Signs for Memphis. Chicago.

The 'Cross of the Crossroads' in Effingham. A stainless-steel leviathan standing at one hundred ninety-eight feet tall and one hundred thirteen feet wide. Forged out of over one hundred eighty tons. A small theater at its Welcome Center shows a video recounting the construction, the narrator proclaiming, *"Until the Lord comes back, and this world comes to an end, the light of this cross is going to shine for people who travel by."*

'You can buy the video, if you like. Make a donation,' quips Jack.

St. Louis appears, the city where I had flown in for basic army training twenty-one years ago. It's hard to believe so much time has gone by. But I can still see that day, fresh and vivid in my mind. Thankfully, I don't feel intimidated by the drill sergeants anymore.

The Mississippi River. Then the arch—Gateway to the West.

Jack and I stopped one time and went up to the top. Cramped in a tiny tram, nothing more than a capsule with no windows, but an astounding view at the top.

The city recedes and the traffic thins. Commercial buildings separate and the farmland returns.

More scruples:

Yahweh's Assembly
This Exit

'Home of the brave. Land of the free. Quite a spectacle.'

Passions Sex Shop This Exit

'Nothing like doing something worthwhile... of great faith,' Jack says.

Bucksnort Trading Co.
Two miles

'Where you can buy all the bullets you want.'

Uranus Fudge Factory
St. Robert, Missouri

'Then, stop by for a knock 'em dead treat,' Jack says with a grimace.
The sun is setting—a deep red, blazing ball.
Eyes burning, back aching, foot cramping.
Time to get off the highway.

The New Way to Pioneer

On I-90 West in the Mustang.

Jack's trusty badge of independence and power. His old, faded red 1987 5.0 Hatchback GT. The Fox body. The lustiest from those years of Ford's attempt to revitalize their signature model of an American symbol.

Originally introduced at the New York World's Fair in 1964, this was the third generation of pony car, and had wild-eyed, wrap around headlights, and a smoother, rounder nose. There was a spoiler too, and a fuel-injected Windsor 4.9 liter (Ford just rounded up), V-8 engine that gave us somewhere between 200 to 300 horsepower, allowing us to prance down the highway as we bootstrapped our way to Yellowstone.

Or should I say gallop?

Used, it wasn't a filly. There were some miles on it. But, like our apartment, it didn't matter. Our steed was tough and rough. Growly and dirty. Testy and ornery. A scrappy, truculent roadster, smeared with dried mud, its temperament only matched by the sheer effervescence of being on the asphalt with it.

As always, Jack was introspectively absorbed. "I've always thought that the highway is a prepackaged experience, not worth the time because there's no originality."

I smiled and nodded as we sped through South Dakota. "I couldn't agree more. Then why are we here?"

"I'll answer you with a little history. Do you know that, starting in 1903, the road trip was officially ushered onto the stage of America's psyche when H. Nelson Jackson and Sewall K. Crocker drove from San Francisco to New York in sixty-three days?"

As we galloped outside of the Badlands, I shook my head. "Nope."

"It's true history. They lumbered along, over and through the once well-trodden, dusty wagon trails of yore in a brand-new Winton Touring Car."

Our wheels spun past the white striped lines, away from the Corn Palace, which we hadn't bothered to stop at this time, despite the insistent signs for one hundred and fifty miles. Or thereabouts.

Jack looked around at the vast landscape. "Their dog, Bud, went with them."

"No shit?" I asked, forever bewildered and intrigued by his seemingly random knowledge. Trivial maybe for some, but never for me. The son of a professor, Jack's preference for speech was often singular, formal, sometimes peculiar, as if his upbringing had instilled a sense that he must always present himself with educated dignity.

"No shit," he replied.

Our worn tires passed a sign which beckoned us to visit the six-ton prairie dog. Nothing like it in the world.

"Did you also know that Alice Huyler Ramsey followed in 1909? She and three companions left Hell's Gate in New York and beat the sixty-three-day tour by four days. Blanche Stuart Scott followed along in 1910."

He took an ambitious bite from his freshly opened egg salad sandwich he had bought at our last "gas up and stretch our legs" break. A Love's Travel Stop.

"Man or woman, road trip fever had begun to take," he stated with an affirmative nod.

"It didn't take long to catch."

"No, it didn't. And never one to let the fun continue without a presence, the federal government soon stepped in and passed the Federal Aid Road Act of 1916, which helped fund the construction of roadways." Another energetic bite. "Soon after, in 1921, the Federal Aid Highway Act was passed, a first effort at constructing a national road grid. Then, in 1926, the numbered highway system was established; it was completed near the end of the thirties. And Route 66 became a primary route for this new tribe of pioneers. Today, it's a national icon and an asphalt pilgrimage for every sort of hodophile imaginable."

I suspected his usual verbal calisthenics were now warming up.

Another mouthful. "And not just for vacations. Everyone's hope for a better life somewhere else also promoted that crazy, new highway spiderweb. Naturally, our country was now on the move, and even more independent because by the 50s more and more families owned cars. They were more reliable, with the time required to travel long distances being reduced to days, not weeks. So, of course, roadside businesses popped up everywhere – restaurants, travel agencies, clothing stores, repair shops, coffee shops; you name it."

I nodded again. "That much is clear."

"The first 7-eleven opened in 1927 in Dallas. Then came along all those gimmicky stops like Wall Drug back there."

"Sounds like nothing more than attractions to check off someone's list," I said with a grimace.

He chuckled, then chomped again. "Oh, come on, Dana. It became the new way to pioneer."

"I see problems in that."

"And you would be right. Like the covered wagon and steam engine era, I think that the primary one was that no one bothered to ask the Native Americans how they felt as they watched all those new Fords, Chevys, Cadillacs—"

"And Oldsmobiles and Pontiacs—"

"and Dodges, Plymouths, and Lincolns rip through the prairies, mountains, and deserts. They had already been sequestered to regions least valued by the government and were rapidly becoming mere curiosities for sightseers. Another picture taking opportunity for the kids while slurping down a milkshake from a roadside diner."

"An orgy of asphalt," I observed.

Another mouthful. "True that. But the real explosion took place shortly after, when Eisenhower initiated the Interstate Highway System. Would you believe it was officially completed, just a few years ago, in '92? Now, we have even more speed, and controlled access, no less. Full circle, the road trip is now so revered that a National Road Trip Day has been established. It ushers in the summer driving season shortly before Memorial Day." He grinned. "Happy smiles for Shell and Exxon."

"Never heard of it."

"Wanna stop at Wall Drug? Get some fries?"

"Seriously dude?"

He polished off the last of the egg salad.

My mind swirled with his observations and opinions. And as I looked out over the vast grassland, a sense of irony washed over me. Irony at my friend's mysterious affection toward convenience store sandwiches while he critiqued highways as a pre-packaged experience.

He was right, of course. More roads, more speed, more of everything meant more complacency, and therefore, a removal and indifference to the Earth and the beings who occupy it.

With his usual uncanny ability, he seemed to sense my thoughts because, after a quick flick of his wrist, the empty, plastic sandwich container was discarded into the back seat, and he answered before I could speak.

"I'm guilty as charged," he said, a sardonic grin spreading across his face.

Suburban Cowboys

Out in the boonies around three a.m.

Off the cuff, like our trip to somewhere, anywhere, and out in the middle of nowhere on some back, two-lane road, we figured we were only a few more hours away, so it wouldn't hurt to get a little shuteye.

We'd do the rest in the morning.

Off the main drag was where we wanted to pitch our tent. Free from the constraints of a legitimate campground crated within the dull bounds of a caravansary experience. In the wild, and really roughing it, while on our way to the Devil's Tower. A few winks would do the trick for our weary bodies and minds. We knew we would be on rancher's land, but the rationale was that by the time we were back on the road, no one would know the better.

Jack slowed, hunched over the steering wheel, and his sharp eyes peered into the darkness. Not long after, perhaps twenty minutes, he gave a cry of excitement. He slammed on the brakes and the Mustang screeched to an angled halt over the yellow-painted lines. Distinctly acrid smoke billowed over our horse and when it cleared, there, in the shadows, barely visible, was a little dirt, side road with a cattle guard.

About a half mile up, we found a nice sandy spot at the bottom of a dry, shallow creek bed. We parked, pitched our tent, unrolled our sleeping bags, and had just begun to drift off when, suddenly, Jack sat straight up.

"What is it?" I gasped.

"Do you hear that?"

I closed my eyes, trying to listen closely. About to shake my head; about to say, "Nah," when I heard it.

A siren way off in the distance. Or what sounded like a siren.

A rise in octave followed by a fall.

Fully awake, we sat there, listening. I felt my heart in my chest. My breath was shallow with small puffs of damp air.

"Whattya think we oughta do?" I asked.

"I suggest we see if it passes. Nobody could've seen us come in here."

"Yeah. But what if they did."

As we listened, we realized it wasn't a siren. We didn't know what it was, only that the night silence began to lend clarity to quality and form. It was closer now, the pitch still rising and falling. A ghostly crooner accompanied by an arpeggio that made our skin crawl.

Closer. Closer.

Closer still.

"It's in front of us, down by the road," Jack stated.

"No, it's not. It's over there," I countered, my finger jabbing the wall of the tent.

Strained, our anxious ears finally perceived reality—discordant carols in the murky darkness. And then it happened. They were on us.

A pack of coyotes.

Twenty of them. No, thirty. Maybe thirty-five.

They pawed at the tent. Snuffled at the ground. Some teeth snapped. A few snips and a yelp. A squealing stutter-squall. They cackled and snickered with delighted curiosity, intent with a tee-hee chortle of menace and aim.

We looked at each other. His eyes wide as a full moon. Mine, the same. Now, my heart pounded and my hands shook. Both of us were at a loss for words. A striking contrast between the silence in the tent and the yammer of jaws outside.

Then, as if a dam broke, we began to holler and beat on the walls of the tent with the flats of our hands. Startled by our raucous tout de suite of panic, an eerie quiet ensued. Some paws dashed away. All of them? Some of them? Or did they? Maybe.

Where were they?

We didn't know and the silence deafened us. My stomach grumbled. Jack unconsciously tapped a finger on his sleeping bag. An eternity passed. Years of our lives were lost as we sat there and wondered if they'd gone. It was only a minute or so.

We looked at each other.

"Let's get the hell out of here," he whispered.

Slowly, Jack leaned forward, reached out an arm, his fingers enclosing the pull tab of the zipper of the tent. "You ready?"

I swallowed a bowling ball, then said, "Okay. Do it."

ZZZ...zip.

Nothing.

No raging horde barreled in. No fur glistered in the beam of the flashlight. No melee arose from sharp claws and pointed choppers.

Without a word, we squeezed around each other in a frantic scramble. Crammed ourselves through the opening and looked around for a second. Feet dirty and with toes that gripped the dewy sand, our two heads twisted back and forth, mirroring each other. The beam from Jack's flashlight flickered over the darkened slopes of the plain.

More silence.

Then, with barely concealed terror kept at bay by a guise of brisk and adept movement, dumb with expediency, we bundled the tent into itself—poles, sleeping bags and everything else piled up inside—and, like two frenzied Djembe players, dropped the unruly mess into the confines of the trunk.

Jack thrust his hand into the pocket of his jeans for the car keys. "Let's make a break for it," he said grimly.

We dove into the Mustang and the engine blasted to life. The headlights pierced the darkness and the rear tires ground up the prairie. Damp swirls of dirt spread behind us as we dashed for Route 191.

Wide awake now, relieved laughter overcame us as we drove north until we found an all-night gas station some miles up the road from our deadly encounter. We decided to pull in for some java and fill up the tank. At the register, on a whim, we asked a heavy-set woman with voluminous breasts about coyotes in the area.

An abridged version of our story soon followed.

The local wisdom set in her eyes warmly mocked us, as if to say, "Good lord, more suburban cowboys." And her faded halter dress—a pattern of fuchsia, white, yellow, and orange flowers—jiggled with a giggle.

She looked at us, scratched her bristly steel wool hair that was tucked in a bun, then shrugged her shoulders, and said categorically, "They ain't nuthin.' They're like crickets 'round here. Most times, they just want to know who's in their territory for the night. Nuthin' to worry about." She paused, brown eyes narrowed, scrutinizing us. A hint of a smirk remained. "They didn't give ya too bad a fright, did they?"

Glances were exchanged all around for a few seconds.

Then, Jack waved his hand through the air with dismissiveness and declared. "No ma'am. We been camping all around these parts for years now and we know the ways of 'em – and any other critter that happens to be in the neighborhood too. Yes, ma'am, inside and out, but no sense provoking 'em, ain't that right, partner?"

His elbow nudged my arm.

I nodded an affirmative. "You know it."

With eyes that never left us, she hoisted her pack of Capri

cigarettes, pulled one out, slowly placed it between her cherry-red painted lips, and lit it with a John Deere green Bic. "Uh, huh. Well, you boys take care now."

"We sure will. And thanks for the coffee."

A few minutes later, with a full tank of gas and tails tucked between our legs, we were back in the Mustang.

At sunup, we pulled into the Homestead Campground and Family Resort.

Gypsy Moths

Like a dreadful alien virus from a science fiction film, uncountable numbers of slender, fuzzy gray bodies with raised red/blue warts slinked not just along trees, but everywhere—outdoor patios, deck furniture, and cars. Lawn mowers, picnic tables, and birdhouses. Some even found shelter in homes. Or a discarded beer can.

Their wispy, white silk tents and black droppings stretched far and wide along the crotches of the branches of trees and shrubs, which made the sumptuous, opulent forests look more like something Jack Finney or Robert Heinlein would dream up. Anyone living in New England during that time in the early 1980s will surely recall the horror.

Not being the first swarm, they had periodically decimated the northeast for years. A long run of outbreaks that dated back to the late 19th century (thank you, Leopold Trouvelot), and defoliated more than ten million acres of woodland over the course of their voracious siege.

This was only the most recent.

Jack and I watched helplessly, along with everyone else, as our rich green nature transformed into an impoverished wasteland.

The trees didn't like it either.

And as a duty to be stewards of the Earth and its fellow inhabitants, our ten-year-old minds had decided to stop this cascade of flocculent foes in their multi-legged tracks on that hot, dry, cloudless day in August 1982.

One of those perfect days of innocent childhood.

We marched into the woods behind my parents' house; the same woods where, four years later, my friend Joey would be shot in the cheek with a BB, the final shot of the so-called Great BB Gun War.

Joey still has the BB in his cheek. Calling me in late 2019, the mirth in his voice was unavoidable as he told me, because of an injury, he was supposed to consent to an MRI, but that the metal pellet was preventing it. The doctors had asked if he ever thought about removing it and were bewildered at his refusal, Joey claiming that it helps him think as he absently rolls it around with the tip of his finger. He's fond of his spherical contemplation.

But back then, his cheek was still free of metal as Jack and I passed by that spot, then tramped further on, back to a grove of oak and maple, with a few birches and hemlock, which surrounded a moderate-sized clearing.

He stopped. I shrugged.

"Well?" he asked.

"Good a place as any, I guess. Gotta start somewhere."

Our idea had been drafted the night before while he slept over. My father, who was the head of maintenance in the Media Department for the local university, had learned that a 16-mm copy of the latest Bill Murray comedy, *Stripes*, had been rented by the students and was still in the campus' film vault. Having access, he had 'borrowed' it for a private showing in the basement of our house. Jack and I were delighted. Not only was it a funny movie which filled our imagination with an Army we'd love to join, with heroes and adventure, but it was R rated. Wide eyes never left the screen as we gawked and giggled at the naked breasts of the women during the now famous mud wrestling scene. My father was the real hero that night. Later, in my bedroom, as we beamed with a new sense of being grown-ups, our plan came together.

"I'll go this way," he declared as he pointed to a nearby oak tree.

"Okay. I'll take over there. Get as many as you can. Meet in the middle of the clearing?"

"Right."

Twenty minutes later we kneeled before a pile of branches laden with nests. I could see the caterpillars through their cottony mist, as they wriggled over each other, upset that their den had been tousled with.

"So how do you want to do this? Do you think we should smoosh them?" Jack asked.

"Nope. I got something better," I grinned as I reached into the front pocket of my navy-blue corduroys and pulled out a book of matches. "I stole them from my mom. She has a whole drawer full of them."

Jack smiled, his eyes alight. "Oh, so cool. Gimme. I wanna light one up."

"Not before me. We do this together."

"Okay."

I opened the book and broke off a match. Two swipes at the striking surface and a bright, orange flame burst to life. I handed the matches to him. On the first try, his was lit. We knelt there, looked at each other, and held our matches. The woods were motionless and quiet. Breathless. I could feel the heat of the sun as it burned into my shoulders and through my hair.

"You ready?"

"Yep. Let's do it."

The nests ignited easily. The silk contracted and dwindled like plastic wrap, shrinking in on itself. Then the branch caught. Then the branches. The caterpillars began to squirm in panicked anguish. They began to catch fire.

Jubilant, we beamed with hubris, stepped back, and slapped each other a high five.

"Awesome," he said.

"Yeah. Die worms."

Jack looked at me. "Yuck. Smells like a moose's ass."

I nodded. "I know, right?"

Smoke began to burn our eyes.

A small breeze, light and airy. Just a puff. But it was enough to hoist an ember of a branch. Threads from a nest still clung to it as Jack and I watched as it was carried away.

Higher and higher; just out of reach.

Our heads swiveled. Our eyes locked in a moment, then shifted downward. Fear seized us like a clamp. It stopped our hearts, squeezed our lungs, made our hands and arms tingle.

"Oh shit," he exclaimed.

The fire hadn't surrendered to our will; hadn't died down. It wasn't concentrated solely on our woolly bear enemies of the forest. Rather, it had built an appetite of its own.

A will of riot and distemper.

A crispy, crimson ring had spread from our pile of branches and, for a moment, I was amazed at how perfectly circular it was.

In awe at perfected, perilous expansion.

Now frantic, Jack and I began to orbit the miscreation. Opposite each other. Two desperate moons around a blazing sun as our feet stomped and thrashed the dried leaves from last autumn. But with each dull thud of our now sooty, blackened Addidas, the air whisked out from underneath.

Our soles only served to widen the burgeoning blaze.

Terror-stricken, I yelled, "I'm gonna go up to the house and get a blanket or something. We gotta smother it."

He didn't look up, his sneakers too busy with the seared tinder. Panicked legs pumped up and down, smoke curling around his body, his head, his face wet with sweat.

Ten or fifteen minutes later, I was back with a clear, plastic tarp I managed to find in my father's tool shed behind the house. But, by then, the fire had widened. Like an incubus conjured from the deepest of nightmares, unleashed, it consumed the entire clearing, the flames beginning to lick the bases of the surrounding trees. Across from the clearing, I watched as the lower branches of a hemlock touched off with sprawled fire.

I could hear them crinkle and crackle.

Snap. Pop.

And see it hiss.

Phizzz.

A *rumble*, then,

snip-snap-whoosh.

Jack ran over to me, grabbed my shirt by the shoulder, and wrenched me toward him. His eyes were obscenely wide. His lips were trembling. We were enveloped in a cloud of gray smoke. It cleared and he screamed into my intensely hot face, "It's hopeless. We gotta call the fire department."

A desperate sprint back to my parents' house ensued. The limbs of yet unburned trees whipped our arms; cut our faces. The roar of the demon we had created lashed our ears with its hateful laughter. Sneakers darted over rocks; bounded over leaves.

We burst through the back door, breathless, and found my mother on the couch in the living room. Relaxed, she was immersed in her latest horror book—*Different Seasons* by Stephen King. She looked up, took in our dirty, sweaty, soot smudged clothes, our blood-streaked cheeks, and arms with sudden alarm. "Lord almighty. What on earth happened? What's going on?" she asked.

"Mom, you gotta call the fire department. The woods are on fire out back," I panted.

Without a word, she leapt up. Her book dropped to the floor, and she raced to the telephone mounted on the wall opposite the couch.

Beep, boop, boop.

"Hello? Nine one one?"

That evening, after not only our own towns, but all the neighboring towns, fire trucks had left, after at least thirty firefighters had gone home, after being questioned about what happened, after being told that a minimum of five acres had been burned, after facing dubious scowls from the department chiefs as we claimed innocence and told lies, after my mother defended us, stated that we were good boys and wouldn't do such a thing, after surviving my mother's own chastising (she knew we were guilty), after my father grounded me, after Jack was picked up by his parents and was lashed with verbal condemnation in his own house, I pulled my bed covers close around me, grasped them in my fingers and tucked them under my chin.

Afraid to close my eyes, I wondered, how could everything have gone so wrong?

Good intentions, it seemed, didn't always work out as planned.

I was guilty as charged.

Sky Fathers

I opened my eyes and every muscle in my body ached. Cramped from sleeping and driving, driving and sleeping. A deep, watery-eyed yawn with legs pressed against the footboard underneath the glove compartment, and hands clasped around the back of the headrest paved the way to some relief.

Bone marrow weariness; an intrinsic part of being on the road.

Jack glanced at me as he reached forward and turned down the radio. "I'm glad you're awake. We're just about in Colorado."

A mumbled question, "What were you listening to?"

"Some sky father's been blathering on about abortion rights. It seems he thinks that Kansas ought to start raising some hell about it."

I closed my eyes, exasperated with the prospect of another talk about social issues, while thinking, *Oh Jesus, here we fuckin' go again. I'm just waking up for God's sake.*

I sighed.

While I loved his thoughtful rhapsodies, respected his viewpoints, and was often happy to be Robin to his Batman, there were times when my mind just didn't want to venture into another mental crusade. Another curbside foray into ideology. But he had a way of coaxing me for reasons I couldn't explain. Perhaps, regardless of how I felt in the moment, I intuitively knew that in the end, I would be intellectually stimulated in a way I hadn't before.

Perhaps I needed them.

"Oh my God, indeed," said Jack, apparently to the radio.

He was quiet for a minute, then turned it off. I could tell he was lost in thought.

He reached between the seats and picked up the roast beef sub he had bought at our last stop—a Flying J Travel Center. His teeth tore through the plastic, peeled it back, and he took a bite of the whole width while his eyes squinted through the low, early afternoon sun. The pale winter sky cloudless.

An audible gulp, then he spoke. "We Americans seem to have this sense of rugged individualism to the extreme, like a stubbornness that we know it all and don't need to be told anything different." Another mouthful. "And we think this makes us exceptional, the greatest country that ever was, or ever will be for that matter."

"I don't know. So, you don't think we're exceptional?"

"Sounds suspiciously like arrogance to me."

"Like those assholes who think they're right about shooting doctors over abortions? That's a shitty way of expressing your love of life."

"Agreed." Another massive swallow. "Personally, I think that our arrogance is born from fear. And people are generally fearful. Good examples are, here come the liberals to take your guns; the commies to take your freedom. There's always some nameless, faceless other launching a war on our way of life."

"Oh, hell Jack, that whole war on freedom bullshit's been a punchline for God knows how long." I yawned again. "Maybe, for them, it all boils down to good guy versus bad guy. Very black and white."

"It's also a myth," he replied. "In hero with a thousand faces, Joseph Campbell said that myth is embedded in all our cultures. Underneath the live and let live rhetoric of everyday, going to work, barbequing America, is a very real feeling that if you're different than us—"

"Then you don't belong," I finished.

Drowsy as I was, I rubbed it out of my eyes. Now, I was immersed in the conversation. And intrigued. Besides, admittedly, I did love the intellectual challenge he posed when we talked about deeper subjects. I felt affirmed and connected. Comforted, as if I wasn't the only one who mused. Who felt uneasy as I tried to exist in a society I felt needed to ask, and maybe answer, some difficult, even inconvenient questions.

I needed this after all.

He nodded. "Funny how our American melting pot has nothing to do with empathizing with others who are different from us."

I looked out the window, at the grain silo we sped by. "The whole thing seems ridiculous, but if you're passionate about something—"

"Bah. You can also look at it this way. A passionate belief, when combined with arrogance, leads to the fear we've been talking about. But no myth in the world will make that belief real."

"Yeah, I get that. And speaking of fear, what about the whole thing about Americans thinking that if you work hard enough you can make it. Whatever that means."

Another gobble. Half of the sub was gone now. "What about it?"

I sighed again, this time with a longing for coffee. "Well, you know the game is rigged, don't you, Jack? Has been for a long time. We have workers and the rich folks, and not much of a middle class. And I'm not sure I can go along with having to push everyone out of the way to be successful."

Now, three quarters of the sub had disappeared. "I *have* thought of that. What's important to understand is that in America, you're either a winner or a loser. Americans are terrified of that, but what makes it all the worse is that the definition of winner is narrow, even oppressive. If you don't become a winner by the standards set in place, then no one deems you important enough. For instance, speaking for an interview. If you're a loser, then your opinion doesn't have as much value to society. Authors who don't have a seal stamped on the front cover of a book aren't worth as much. You're not worth reading." He took another bite, then looked at me. "If you *do* become an author, be sure that you do it for the craft of writing."

"Definitely. I'm not really the ruthless type anyway."

He finished the rest of his sandwich and sat back. A full-toned, contented belly-belch reverberated through the car cabin. "I guess everybody has their own reality, bro. However arrogant it may be, I just want mine to count for something. And you should too."

I turned to him. "Coincidentally, this all goes along with that going west thing we've talked about, you know that, right?"

"Not such a coincidence. You ever notice how when you're driving west, you can outrun the sun?"

"What do you mean?"

"Well, if you drive fast enough, you can prolong the day because you're going west. It takes longer for the sun to set, so you're actually catching up with it."

Astounded at this sudden change of topic, I didn't know what to say. I could tell by the look on his face, the frown, and the distant look in his eyes, that he was obviously troubled by this last thought.

Somehow. Someway.

An inward trouble.

And for the first time, in all the years I had known him, I realized that he seemed disconnected somehow. That there was something more than merely his mind running circles with his logic. It was as if the voice who was speaking couldn't convince him. As if he was aware he had knowledge, but weakness too. Acceptance, but inability. Wisdom, but laziness. Something he couldn't put his finger on, yet knew was there.

Always out of reach. Forever elusive.

Something he couldn't let go of.

I wished I could say something more profound, something

meaningful, something to connect us, and thereby help him to connect inwardly. But, in all reality, it was a trouble that there was nothing I could do to help him with.

And I felt a deep sadness.

Feeling helplessly inept, I said, "Never really thought about it."

He grinned. "That's what you have me for."

Because of a Bullet

Right now, here in the broad, seemingly timeless expanse of Kansas, about one hundred miles from the Colorado border, I'm ruminating.

How long had he planned the last day of his life? Months? Weeks? Days? A moment? Did he get up early? Late? Or did he stay up all night? I don't know if he ate a hearty breakfast—coffee, eggs, bacon, and toast. Or did he do it on an empty stomach? Did he bother to brush his teeth? To use mouthwash? Did he rinse well? I don't know if he wore something special, or just his regular jeans and T-shirt. What was the weather like? Sunny and warm or rainy and cold? And I wonder what his feelings were that morning. Was he numb? Beyond angry? On the other side of sadness? Out of reach of resignation? Or bound to determination?

Did anything earthly matter?

My head swivels for a moment as a black Mustang roars past, heading east on the other side of the highway. Jack's was red.

A lump in my throat.

That morning, as he left his new one-bedroom apartment in Denver, what was the drive like? Was the window rolled down? Did he stop for gas? Did the radio blare? Did he get caught in traffic? Did he watch the people around him—some in cars, some walking the streets—and wonder what they were doing? Did he feel isolated and alone as they led their individual lives, carried on with the piety of their purpose, persisted with the arrogance of their principles, while his crumbled? Maybe he didn't care what those people were doing. I know I didn't. Maybe he thought they were slaves to a machine of which he was no longer a part. I know I did.

The machine, and with it, the meaning of daily life. Occupied and satisfied with their routines—wake up, go to work, take a break, go back to work, eat lunch, go back to work, take another break, go back to work, leave work, stop at a grocery store, eat dinner, watch TV—all the while hypnotized in pointless doomscrolling. Why be a part of their profoundly bottomless scurrying?

Uncomfortable, I wiggle in my seat.

And I wonder if he witnessed all those people, so vital and animated, and he wasn't. Maybe he saw them fulfilling their dreams and desires, and he couldn't. Maybe he saw them appreciating the smallest of daily moments—the smell of home, a cold beer at a picnic—and he didn't. When did the solace of, *I can always take this way out*, become metalized?

I pass an exit for some town I've never heard of, and my stomach quivers.

There are more than a dozen downtown stop lights to reach the outskirts of the city, miles of highway and secondary roads to get into the mountains and reach the open space of White Ranch.

Libby said the police found his note on the driver's seat, where he parked at the trail's head. Did he write it the night before? Weeks before? Or right there behind the wheel?

As he shut the door of his SUV, or on his hike to the meadow where he was married, there was still a chance to turn around. All he had to do was get back in the car or walk back down the mountain. But he wouldn't or couldn't. And didn't.

Amid this beauty and grandeur of wilderness, did he pace for a while? Did he sit and reflect? If he did, for how long? Into the afternoon or all the way through to the last splashes of golden sunshine?

And I wonder why the tranquility of a meadow—among the Ponderosa Pines, Colorado blue columbines, and song sparrows—where he always felt at home, didn't give him pause.

And I don't know why my lifelong friend didn't reach out to talk with me. To confide in me. To ask for help, reassurance, and comfort.

And I don't know his final thought.

Did he finish it?

Or was it cut off in mid—

Crack.

Because a bullet tears through uncertainty with a wet, deafening blast.

Fun with Firecrackers

Bwoom.

The firecracker exploded.

He cheered as he knelt in the sandy dirt. A whoop and a holler that seemed to whistle over the still pond, through the trees, and aloft, into the sky beyond. Rippled through the woods behind our houses, where I found him on my way over to visit. A fierce gleam radiated in his eyes—brighter than the scorched summer sun overhead—and bored into mine.

A gleam which left me both frightened and stupefied. Frightened at the intensity, and the anger I saw. Stupefied because I didn't know what to do. What to make of my best friend. He snatched another Lady Finger out of the pile next to him.

"Stop it, Jack."

"Why? I'm not hurting anyone."

"But you're hurting them."

"They don't even know it."

"Yes, they do."

"How do you know?"

"Because I know."

He shook his head. "No, you don't."

Bwoom.

Firecrackers attached to an old action figure or model can be fun. And the bigger the firecracker, the more intricate the model, the more fun it will be. What young boy hasn't wrapped a string of Black Cats around an old Army sergeant action figure? Or slung an M-80 to a plastic *Millennium Falcon*? Or an old F-18 fighter jet? Like the Crosman 760 Powermaster BB gun I cradled in my arms, it's some sort of weird rite of passage that every red-blooded American boy must go through.

But right then, my voice quivered with fear and rage. "Stop it, Jack. I mean it."

"Make me," he growled without looking up.

Immobilized because I didn't want to fight with him, I teetered. He's my best friend. What do I do? How could he do this?

I fought for belief; for conviction. Then, in desperation, and from a desire to stop the slaughter, unable to come up with anything else that might have been workable, I aimed my BB gun at him.

"Jack, if you don't stop right now, I – I won't talk to you ever again."

He looked up, took in my jittery twelve-year-old arms as the BB gun wavered, the barrel unsteady, and I saw the bright anger of his blue/gray eyes dim for a second. It dimmed to a deep and penetrated sadness. Then, as if I had imagined it, the destructive gleam returned, and he grabbed the large Ziplock on the ground in front of him. He yanked it open and carefully extracted a frog from the mass of slick bodies, bulged eyes, and small arms and legs that frantically kicked at one another. Each scrambled over the others, fought for air, desperate for release; for freedom from the sealed, clear plastic heat dome.

"Yes, you will."

He shoved a Lady Finger in the disoriented, bewildered frog's mouth, lit the fuse with a Bic, then tossed it, and the Lady Finger, on the ground in front of him.

Bwoom.

Then, he calmly picked up his own BB gun from the ground next to him.

And we stared at each other over our respective barrels.

Significant Insignificance

Jack always felt the need to rush through the Great Plains.

For him, the sentiment was that it was boring; lifeless with nothing to do. A vast wasteland that was simply something to get over and done with. And as an amusement for himself, an effort to alleviate the tedium, on one trip he taught me how to draft semis, all the while talking about how it provided him with a psychological feeling that he was going faster. That the miles were less painful.

I feel the opposite. I've always found the plains to be wide open and beyond me in a way that can't be verbalized. Tranquil with an instilled sense that I'm real and infinitesimal in something so large, I can't comprehend.

Significant insignificance.

One time, I made him stop so I could stand in the grass next to the highway. My whole body felt energized, yet infinitesimally small as I spread my arms and closed my eyes next to a lone tree. I felt alive and connected to everything around me, below me, above me, and out of reach.

As I did my thing, I remember Jack sitting on the car hood, watching the semis rumble past. And when I returned and he asked me what I had been doing, all I could say was that, breathing in those minutes gave me perspective on the world and the universe we live in. That I felt joined on the far side of my insides.

He nodded, but didn't say anything.

Later, while eating a tuna salad sandwich he'd bought at the last gas station, he turned to me and said, "I guess I can see your point. You can almost forget who you are when you're here. Almost. And if you can't be free of this world, you have to free yourself internally and spiritually. And places like this can let you find a space so deep inside, that you can't help but be freed."

Now, the expanse of prairie is behind me. And as much as I've gotten my second wind; as much as I'm starting to enjoy being back on the road, I didn't stop this time. I couldn't. I'm too impatient. I'm simply not at peace in my heart with the significance of what looms over the near horizon to consider standing in the grass.

I just need to cross the border into Colorado.

And I'm all too aware that Jack felt insignificant enough to free himself.

Interlude, Part Two – Boot Hill

Overhead, I heard a distorted whistle.

An arched whine.

Instinctively, I winced with the expectation of what was to come.

Bwoom.

The explosion pealed through me; past me. Echoed off the outside of the cells. Bounced back and corkscrewed around my body as it nearly knocked me over. Pebbles rattled as they hopped on the ground that heaved once under my feet. Clumps of sun-hardened sand and gravel from the housing area clattered around me.

The air was thick with dust. Debris.

Bwoom. Bwoom. Bwoom.

The attack seems to go on forever.

Pap, pap, pap.

I have to get out of here.

No power to the Hooches that night; and there's no moon to help see in the darkness of the Iraqi desert night. Only the flashes of the mortar explosions. And, like my father before me, during the Korean War, the red tinted lens of my Army-issued olive-drab flashlight illuminated a letter:

Dana,

This is the only means with which I have to write to you as I am out in the mountains, at camp with the Forest Service. I'm sitting here on a rock, watching the sunset, a welcome hiatus after a long week. I'm tired, dirty and ripe enough to scare away a bear, and I only have a day before we pack up and head to another area where another fire has broken out. I wish you could be here to watch the evening develop. Such an awe-inspiring sight.

While I'm reasonably happy in my life at the moment (things are going well within my relationship with Libby and, despite the smoke in my lungs, this job has exceeded all my expectations for adventure), my worry for your well-being during this difficult phase in your life is much more consuming. I worry about how you're faring as you endure the great game of life and death our government sent you on, and as it were, the roll of the dice with which you may or may not come home to us. Don't be upset with me; I realize it's not a game. I'm phrasing my concern this way for a reason.

Do you remember when we were kids, and we used to play Boot Hill? Remember when the other kids and I would never let you play and always insisted on you being the DM? There was good reason for that. It was because you had the best imaginative powers to invent an adventure for us to go on. None of us could make up stories the way you did. You were so good at it.

I need you right now, while you're immersed in a tap dance of keeping your sanity and staying alive, to find asylum within your imagination. Use that vivid, lively imagination that you've always had to get through this ordeal. The imagination that allows you to invent such interesting, compelling, and textured stories. In other words, the author in you.

When you're being attacked and are afraid, turn to your imagination. Go to your original self, that self of childhood to see you through the madness, that time and space to keep you safe and insulated from the violence surrounding you. As when we were kids.

When you find yourself there, please do take comfort that I'm with you. No matter where we are, no matter what we are doing, no matter the time of day, we are always with each other. Connected in some way beyond friendship, beyond time and space. And beyond that time and space, you will get through this.

I love you, my brother,

Jack

I closed my eyes and gripped Jack's letter tight between my fingers.

Boot Hill.

I saw myself as I walked the streets of a wild, wild west town. Among the scallywags of every type with eyes that glowed with greed; their wide-brimmed hats, grizzled faces, and prickly whiskers. The desert dust, stale smoke from cigars.

A five-ton rumbled by, but was drowned out by the clomp of hooves. The yells around the Hooches became the shrill canticle of spurs. The crunch of combat boots over gravel were only thuds on aged, wooden planks.

And the mortars and gunfire, the fear and violence, were suddenly insignificant.

Roadkill

"Why do you swerve for roadkill?" I challenged Jack, as the Mustang veered sharply to the left, then returned back to its lane. The two-lane road with its grand, panoramic view of the desert. I swiveled my head and watched the lucky prairie dog skittle into a patch of scrub brush.

"Why would I not?"

I turned back to Jack. "Because it's already dead."

"Not that one, but so what?"

"Well—"

"Well, nothing. Do you feel I should blatantly run over a formerly living being because I couldn't be bothered to turn the wheel for a moment?"

"No, that's not what I'm asking."

"What *are* you asking?"

"I'm just wondering why you do it. You personally."

He looked at me, his eyes sharp; that piercing gaze. "I'm more than happy to tell you why but let me ask *you* a question."

"Okay, shoot."

"What do you suppose is the difference between people and animals?"

"Not much, in all reality, I suppose."

"Exactly. Here's how I see it. People tend to make a distinction with just our everyday language – the word people, the word animal. Just that little verbal gesture is the beginning of our mental segregation from nature. And I think that's due to our religious beliefs because, astonishingly enough, we feel we are God's divine creation. Stewards of the Earth, so to speak. But in all reality, we're no better than our fellow creatures – and in some ways, we could very well be worse."

"I see."

"So, to answer your question about roadkill, let me ask you this. Why do we, as people, who claim to value life and honor death, feel so indifferent to running over the corpse of one of our fellow beings on the highway? We wouldn't do that if a human was lying there. At least, no one I would want to associate with. What makes their lives less valuable than ours? Because they don't speak our language? Hogwash. We don't speak theirs either. Don't we all have to eat, drink, piss, shit, and sleep? We all want shelter. Warmth. A sense of belonging. We all desire love, possess awareness, and engage in a social life. We all strive for cleanliness, have a voice, and can recognize faces. Plus, along with all our fears and doubts, our wants and needs, we all feel pain. We're all vulnerable to disease and finally, absolutely everything has a will to live. Even a virus."

A memory began to flash through my mind. "A virus?"

"Yes, a virus. Many think that *we* are the ultimate virus on this planet," Jack speculated.

"Can't say that I blame them. But hold on a second."

"Yes?"

"Now, don't get all pissy with me, or upset or anything, but do you remember when we were kids, and I caught you blowing up those frogs?"

He glanced at me, wary of what I was going to say next. "Yes?" he repeated.

"Well, so, you were killing them. Putting firecrackers in their mouths. What's so different now?"

He paused and glanced around at the vast, scrubby expanse; the sunbaked rusty buttes and mesas of New Mexico. Past the Guadalope Mountains—just about the epitome of nowhere. The exception being U.S. Route 50 in Nevada, dubbed the loneliest road in America. Or Interstate 70 east of Green River in Utah and into Colorado. But lonely is too small a word for these vast neighborhoods. And comfortless, I'm sure, for the aliens who crashed near Roswell in 1947. Not that they were particularly interested in the company of humans.

Neither were we. Southeast of Albuquerque, we were on the road to Carlsbad Caverns National Park. Determined and never willing to back down from an adventure, the caverns weren't an easy place to visit. The nearest semblance of civilization was at least forty miles or more away in any direction. Hiking and camping bare bones were literally all there was to do. And the empty silence, with only the wind, was your only companion. Other than Jack, me, and our tent. Perfect, the ambience never failed to take my breath away.

"I can sum it up for you in two words – well, three – age, experience, and reflection."

"So, you feel as if you've changed?"

"Obviously. I've become humbler as we've gotten older. And I've had a chance to think about why I did those things, and how wrong they were. You were right to try and stop me."

I couldn't help but interrupt him, the memory of being chased through the woods—a shootout until exhaustion took hold—salient for me. "I felt like we were going to kill each other that day." I paused, and there was silence between us, then, "But you and I burned the Gypsy Moths too. Remember that?"

"Of course I do. Which brings me back to what I was saying. It's funny, in a not so funny hah hah way, how we even made a distinction between the frogs and the caterpillars with our ceaseless desire to categorize, with us on top of course; killing different creatures who *all* have a right to exist on this planet. Interesting how we're slow to grasp these concepts. There's no humility. No sense of interdependence. No balance."

"I think that balance is the key word in what you said, Jack. It seems to me that everything is a balance in life."

"Agreed."

"You got a smoke?"

Jack nodded toward me "The fiberglass filtered cancer sticks are in the center console."

Drowned Rat

Lazy like the water, my gaze drifted over the silvery Arkansas River as we neared the Royal Gorge. Floating like the reflected sun on the gentle undulation.

Up and down. Up and down.

The raft was stable, even with the slight bob, so I allowed my lids to close; allowed myself a serene repose.

Splish.

A curly sprinkle of icebox water doused my face.

"Wake up there, sleepy head. We be pulling over for the night."

I wiped the water from my face, and sat up, looking around through the hot, summer sun. "Did I fall asleep?"

"You sure did. Not that I blame you. This river is so tranquil, I was starting to get drowsy myself."

Cross-legged and cramped from the small confines of the gray rubber raft, I tried to straighten my legs, but instant fire shot through them. I looked down at the flamed redness of my knees, knees which matched the color of my life preserver vest, then to the left where Jack sat opposite me, his oar resting on his lap. A grimace of consternation was spread over his face.

"From the looks of you, it might not be a bad idea to cool you down," he suggested.

The raft glided to a stop on a sandy embankment about fifty

yards wide, and the four of us clambered out—Noah, Oliver, Jack, and me. With oars stowed, we all began to unload the raft of our equipment and supplies. Me with awkward lurches as my toes gripped the hot sand, hobbled and stumbling with tight, hot pain.

Jack clapped his hands together and rubbed them with vigor. "Fan-fucking-tastic! I can't wait."

"You might say otherwise after tomorrow," said Noah as he pulled a mess kit from his backpack.

"Never."

Everyone laughed.

Oliver disappeared into the wilderness as he called over his shoulder. "I'll get some wood for the fire."

"We'll set up the tent," proposed Jack. "Right after I take care of our injured."

Noah unzipped the front pocket of his pack and produced a white tube. "Here use this, it's aloe. It'll help soothe the pain. Told you, you should've used sunscreen."

I nodded, then sighed as I slumped to the ground and rested my back on a damp log, my body grateful for the cool of the wood. "I know. You were right."

Jack took the aloe and kneeled to the side of my legs. He looked me over for a moment with a mental diagnosis, then unscrewed the cap. "Oh boy. Doesn't look pretty." Then, he smiled. "But don't you worry, brother, ol' doc Jack is here, and he'll fix you up."

He squeezed some of the aloe onto the palm of his hand, then began to gently massage it into my left knee. I winced.

"You okay?" he inquired. "Not too much pressure?"

"Yeah – yeah, I'm okay." I paused. "I'm so stupid, Jack."

He stopped and looked at me. A frown grew on his face. "Humbug," he replied as he began to massage the other knee.

"I am. I should've known and listened. Being on the river, the water reflecting the sun all day. What an asshole I am. I shouldn't have come with you guys."

He stopped for a second time. His voice lowered, intensely serious. "Don't you ever say that about yourself. Just because you got a nasty burn today doesn't make you stupid."

I winced.

"Besides, you see things about people that most don't want to – or can't. And you're far smarter, kinder, funny, creative, and thoughtful than *I* could ever hope to be."

"Bullshit."

"Bullshit my ass. Someday I hope you use those talents of yours; like being an author. Better yet, you *need* to. You have wisdom you can use to enlighten others – and the creativity to put it on paper. You can balance out the craziness out there with your insights." He grinned. "Plus, this is *our* adventure."

I stared at him for a long moment, the heat from my sunburn now replaced by the warmth of my heart. "Thanks, Jack. Someday, I hope I can do the same for you."

A nourisher, Jack always put others first. As if he lived by the time-honored axiom—the needs of the many outweigh the needs of the few. Or the one. And despite me being eight months older, I always had the sense that he felt a first-born fraternal toward me. A big brother who had my back no matter what.

He shrugged. "Not a problem." He leaned back and wiped his hands on his shorts. "Is that better?"

I sighed heavily. "Yeah."

He winked. "Then let's have a beer and enjoy the evening."

○

The next morning, under a bright Colorado sun, we packed up the campsite and went back on the river. The tranquility of yesterday was soon behind us, as the front of the raft began to bob up and down. And per Noah's prediction, we quickly reached the rapids. Now, spray rushed over and around the gray heads of the rocks that poked through the water.

Jack had taken his usual front seat on the left of the raft.

I sat by his elbow.

"Should we be doing this?" I asked Jack as I dipped my paddle into the clear water and glanced down at my aloe white thighs.

He glanced over at me, his own paddle in sync with mine. "Of course we should. There's nothing to be afraid of. It's only a river."

His words didn't particularly console me.

But as my teeth clenched and I felt my pulse quicken in my chest, my neck, my arms, and my battered legs, I knew there was no turning back. I knew I had to face this or cower in the puddled bottom of the raft.

The latter wasn't an option.

With a big gulp of air, I focused my eyes on what lay ahead of us. The other guys didn't matter anymore. In my mind, only Jack and I were here, determined to conquer mother nature's intent. And nothing could stop us.

I took another deep breath and willed my mind to center. Forced myself to go with the flow. And after a moment, a profound calm washed over me. I could resist the current or allow it to carry me. I embraced my fate.

I was in the raft. With the raft. I was the raft.

And I began to enjoy the ride.

"Remember," declared Noah over the roar of the water, "follow my commands. And if you get thrown over, relax. Keep your feet in front of you and let your body go loose. You don't want to stiffen up if you hit a rock. You'll likely break a leg or something. And *don't* panic. We'll get you back, don't worry."

The front of the raft bowed to the river. Up, then down…down, then up…then up some more, and then back down. Ever deeper and more energetic. Acute with agitated fury. Disparate with the motionless banks on either side of us.

Aspens with a few scattered lodgepoles silently observed our passage. A touch of Silky Lupine reached my nostrils, carried on the late morning breeze. Sweet. Candied honey-grape. Fresh, galvanized reassurance.

I was ready.

I tightened my grip on the paddle and ballooned my chest. Life jacket tight. Straps locked in place. A small wiggle of my butt. Feet planted firmly in front of me.

No, I wasn't ready.

"Left back paddle – *now*," yelled Noah.

The river unleashed every liquid ounce of its acrimony. Belligerent, single-minded, and allied with the rocks thrusting their heads above the tossed, upheaved water. Waves crashed over the sides. The thunder of the water bellowed in our ears. Now the raft was far past the point of bobbing. Now, it bucked with such intensity, it seemed as if every second it would burst from the pressure.

Up, then down. A tilt. A tip. Down and up.

A lunge.

In unison, we were all slammed from one side, then to the other. If it weren't for the sun overhead, I would've sworn we had entered a typhoon. An image of Odysseus clinging to a mast hovered before me, then was gone.

I turned my soaked face to Jack and, through my half-blinded eyes, I saw him paddling furiously, his lips curled back into a tenacious snarl. The raft swung left, and I cringed. Like the tooth from a shark lying on its back, a boulder jutted from the river.

It was the size of a car. No, a bus.

"Back paddle," bellowed Noah over the cannonade that besieged us.

"Oh shit," yelled Oliver.

"Right back paddle – *now*," screamed Noah.

"Too late," cried Jack.

"High side," shouted Noah.

Thuwump.

The raft slid up the flat side of the boulder.

Up and up and up…up to the top. Then…a hovering sensation, as if we balanced on a tightrope. Suspended by the crash of the water with time stopped. Not a tick or a tock. An interminable moment. But it was exactly long enough for me to be pitched.

Splash.

I was outside the raft. Without the raft. I was definitely not the raft.

I was the river.

Panic. Body and mind out of control. Humbled before the power of water. Dependent upon its good graces to set me free.

Subordinate and defenseless.

Arms and legs flailed. First, a glimpse of benign green trees and blue sky. Next, thousands of gallons of malignant spray. Then, swallowed into the muted, opaque chill surrounded by bubbles that reached for the surface.

A clouded gurgle.

The clamor of the river as I burst from the depths.

My eyes blinked furiously. Water shot up my nose, and I had an urge to sneeze. My life jacket was hunched up under my armpits. I was being slapped in the face by the churned, rageful water. I shook my head and gulped for air.

There was none.

I gulped in water. Too much. My throat contracted with a choked cough. And my stomach convulsed as I was tossed helplessly. A soggy noodle with no wall to stick to.

No time to think. No legs forward. No shore to reach.

The raft out of sight, I was lost in tumbled solid liquid.

I'm drowning.

Back under the water, enveloped darkness, there was a sudden flash of sunlight—and something firm bumped my head. A minute long second, and my life jacket was yanked painfully up into my armpits.

I saw a face. A face with a grin as I was hauled from the now tranquil river back into the safety of the raft.

"Welcome back, partner," chuckled Jack, his arm around me. "You're okay. I've got you." He looked at me and grinned, "How's our drowned rat?"

The Drury Inn

"Welcome to the Drury Inn," she says. "How can I help you?"

My out-of-gas eyes wander over the lobby. "Well, if you don't mind, if you have a room, I'd really like one for the night."

"Of course. Are you traveling with anyone?"

"Nope. Just me."

"Great. And how many nights will you be staying with us?"

"Just tonight – well maybe two. Probably two. Yeah, tonight and tomorrow night. But then I have to hit the road."

"Let me see what I have. May I offer you a complimentary beer?"

My eyes light up. A complimentary beer! I'm not used to being treated this way. And it delights me. "Oh yeah. That'd be great. Thank you so much."

"Not a problem."

She points across the lobby to the dining/lounge area where thirty other people are milling around or sitting in plush, cushioned chairs at circular, faux walnut stained tables. The adults are drinking; the kids are eating ice cream. All of them are talking and laughing. The remaining sunlight filtering through the high glass windows makes their faces look as though they were awarded a group discount on fake tans.

"Just see the bartender over there and tell him you're checking in, then come back here and your room should be ready."

"Thank you. Won't be but a minute."

"I'll be right here."

"Oh, is there a place to grab a bite to eat around here?"

"Of course. Across the parking lot there's a Jersey Mike's. Their sandwiches are wonderful. And tomorrow morning, we'll have a full breakfast available in the dining room."

Later, after paying, and visiting the sub shop, I bring my bags up to my fifth-floor room. The ultra-modern elevator surprises and amuses me with its soothingly pleasant, female, robotic courtesy voice gliding from the tiny overhead speaker—

"Going up."

"Are you now?" I ask with a wink.

Swish.

Clump, whir, clump.

A monotonal *ding.*

Swish.

"Fifth floor."

"Thanks. I knew that."

And now, I'm sitting in one of the silken, plush armchairs in front of the floor-to-ceiling, room wide window, eating a foot-long roast beef sub with everything on it. As I gaze out at the Rockies, I can't help but recognize, now that I'm older, that I appreciate this comfortable accommodation.

I'm too old for ants and sewers, tents and coyotes.

The last sliver of sun winks out behind the mountains, leaving in its wake a scabrous outline capped with bright orange that dissolves into a dark, purple sky. And somewhere up there, beyond the city limits, amid the tall timber with the empty, bottomless wind, Jack's body was found by a random, passing hiker.

Again, I have the nagging sense that somehow, I failed him.

I look at the silken, plush armchair next to me. To Jack, who's also gazing at the fading mountains. He's looking somewhere beyond the horizon. Into the skyline.

Distant.

Lost in thought.

'A sense of failure is not being able to imagine anymore. It's when you forget who you are,' he murmurs, then leans his head back, closing his eyes.

Outrunning the Sun

We were in the Mustang flying past Cheyenne and Francis E. Warren Air Force Base—one of three strategic missile bases in the United States. Its display of replica intercontinental ballistic missiles spread over the flat grass of the entrance—a Minuteman I, a Minuteman III, a Peacekeeper. Towers of phallic, government funded indiscriminate murder. Past Tree Rock. And Buford, the smallest town in America. A puny denizen of one.

Past the Abraham Lincoln Memorial Monument in Laramie, which is basically a big head with a big beard on a big rock standing tall amid the bigness of the plains.

Past Elk Mountain, Red Desert, and Point of Rocks, where they proudly serve miners.

The Grateful Dead in the CD player again. "Mississippi Half-Step Uptown Toodeloo," another of Jack's favorite songs, as we cruised at seventy-five miles per hour.

'On the day that I was born, Daddy sat down and cried…'

Jack turned up the volume and I glanced at the man next to me. I'm not sure if it was a trick of the light, or a scent in the air, but without warning, I was startled to envisage the boy I grew up with. Late one evening when we were eleven as we overheard Jack's father from the living room.

A dinner party with my parents.

"Jack is awkward, in more ways than one. Unlike his brother, he's not very bright. He needs to be treated accordingly."

My friend, the boy, who quietly cried himself to sleep that night after his father yelled at him for what was only a minor infraction. After he crawled into his bed. After I slunk into my sleeping bag next to him and rolled over to face the wall to give him privacy. Neither of us wanted to talk in the darkness of the bedroom.

I heard him cry, but didn't know what to say.

Back in the present, I watched him toss the empty package from an egg salad sandwich over his shoulder. Added to the detritus of discarded wrappers on the back seat—ham and cheese, burritos, a few coffee cups, copies of *Popular Mechanics*, and crumpled issues of *The Onion*.

Another convenience store snack, this time from a Love's Travel Stop.

He opened the quart carton of Tropicana orange juice that had been resting between his legs, and his Adam's Apple bobbed as he took long gulps from it. With the liquid sunshine back in its place between his knees, he pointed to the horizon, then turned down the volume. "We've been outrunning the sun pretty good. Did you notice how long it's taking for it to set?" he asked.

"Yep, I have. Pretty cool."

And my mind lingered once more on the boy. Always a desire to outrun the sun. Even when present, here with me, some part of him elsewhere. Some part of him was always behind us or in front of us. I never knew which or why. Or maybe I did but shrugged it off. Banal complacency that nothing troubled him.

Did that make him a rock I relied on without a second thought?

"Not going to last that much longer though. Rock Springs is coming up soon. That's where we turn off eighty and take one ninety-one north into Yellowstone."

"Well, you're driving. Can't say I'll mind getting off the highway though."

"Amen to that."

"Should we find a place to camp out soon?"

"I think so. We can get a good start in the morning."

We both gazed out at the conflagration of color before us. Wisps of orange clouds. A fiery ball. A silky, smooth collusion of sky burst without heat.

"You know, you can't really outrun the sun. You *do* know that, right?" I proposed.

He looked at me, a faint scowl etched across his lips. "Horsefeathers."

He stepped on the gas, his sudden decision and the acceleration, startling me.

Eighty miles per hour.

I looked over at him and saw his face was tight; concentrated, his eyes focused straight ahead, hands tightly gripping the wheel.

Eighty-five miles per hour.

My heart pounded as I wondered what he was doing.

Ninety miles per hour.

I grabbed the 'Oh my God' bar.

One hundred miles per hour.

The prairie was a blur, nothing but a brushstroke of green grass. And my feet pressed forward on the floorboard, heels down. My thighs tensed. My hand was cramped.

One hundred and ten miles per hour.

The engine roared. An ear split drone.

One hundred twenty miles per hour.

And I began to feel a light lift, as if hoisted. Jacked up by the air underneath. The Mustang's frenetic hooves barely touched the asphalt anymore. I watched in excited terror as the smeared white lane lines began to drift toward the center of the hood. The back end swung out. Not a lot, but enough to feel it in the seat.

One hundred thirty miles per hour.

Then, Jack's foot eased.

The Mustang settled to ninety-five.

Hooves back on the ground.

A minute or so later, he pointed, "That's our exit."

A sharp application of screeching brakes.

A tug of the reins.

As we pulled off the highway, he turned to me and said, "We beat the sun, brother." Then, in a quiet, sardonic tone, "At least I can drive."

Chess, Part One

There's nothing like outdoor living. Bedding down in no-man's land. Bivouacking in the outback, you're out on the range. Nothing like being a cowboy at large. Pushing a Stetson back on a dusty head. Clenching straw between gritty teeth, you're grasping the reins under a vast sky.

Just imagine breathing the fresh air and losing your sense of space in the vast domain of stars. The crackling of burning wood is singing in your ears.

Just imagine leaning back against a rock and dipping your ears in a melody from a sorrowful harp. The breeze is chilling the back of your neck while the fire's warming your face.

Just imagine whittling a spoon from the branch of a tree and listening to a small, cast-iron pan of beans beginning to bubble. A lone coyote is howling in the distance while a Tumbleweed rolls by.

You're roughing it.

You're loving it.

At an RV park outside Rock Springs, Wyoming.

We were seated at a picnic table, under the glare of a fluorescent light mounted on a telephone pole, right off the exit from Interstate 80 and U.S. Route 191. A quarter mile from a fuel refinery with its cluster of above ground storage tanks, near a 24-hour Flying J Travel Center where tankers, semis, and family campers passed through on a continual basis. A freshly delivered large, pepperoni/mushroom pizza open in its box next to our chessboard, along with a six-pack of beer from the park's small grocery store.

Jack's swirly glass pot pipe passed between us.

There's nothing like living off the grid.

Conscious of the spin, I forced my eyes wider in an effort to focus. A permanent grin spread across my face as eagerness to relax and indulge in conversation, without Jack's orbiting logic, bloomed. It also eased the frustration that had grown in my belly from another chess game.

"Have you ever wondered why they name nursing homes 'assisted living facilities'?" I asked. "Even apartment complexes with such breezy, ridiculous names that have nothing to do with the actual environment?"

The pot had worked its way into both of us.

Jack laughed, a gleeful giggle barely in control. "Not really. But now that you mention it, they are flowery, aren't they?" He lowered his voice. "Too flowery."

I picked up the pipe and took another hit, then moved my king one space away from his rook. "Is it supposed to be comforting? To make someone feel better in some mysterious way, for when you're moving in?"

He shrugged. "Maybe." Then he moved a rook to one row before the first one. "Check."

I leaned forward. "Seriously?"

"Come visit Whispering Willows, your peaceful meadow escape from it all," he said.

Concentration on my king was rapidly losing significance. "How about Green Meadows?" I suggested with a grin.

"Well, it's better than One Foot in the Grave. Which is where your king is."

"Fuck you." With marijuana induced reckless abandon, I moved my king to the only safe spot I could think of. "Or how about The Ultimate Escape from Life?"

He moved his first rook. "Or Straddling the Grim Reaper. Check."

I stared at him. He stared at me.

Then together we burst into laughter.

The usual feeling of hopelessness whenever I played chess with him devoured me. I moved my king for a second time. "Nature's Reminder."

He moved his rook again. "Your Expressway to a New Adventure. Checkmate."

"Shit. How does that always happen?"

He shrugged, then took another hit. "Your turn to set up the board. How about End of the Road Retirement Home?"

Gathering up the pieces, I reset the game. "Rusted Years Chateau."

"Heaven's Gate Retirement Home."

"The Aging Birch Terrace."

"Venerable Village."

"El Diablo Villa."

"You go first. Casa Flor Marchita," he said through a bite of pepperoni and cheese.

I moved my first pawn one space forward. "What?"

"Wilted Flower," he said. He moved his first pawn.

I moved another pawn. "Wow, dude."

"Geezer Gardens."

"Imagine what the topiary's like."

"Vertigo Manor."

"Coronary Acres."

"Catheter Estates."

I sat back and thought for a minute. Then, attempting to be witty, I said, "That's on Cemetery Road, isn't it?"

But he was always quicker than me. At least two steps ahead, in thought as well as chess, which his father had taught him to play since we were ten. "Nah, it's a dead end. No outlet." Another pawn.

"The Colossal Cyst Chateau."

A soured look on his lips, puckered. "Okay, I'm good." His queen slid into action.

"Give me a minute," I said. I held my breath, then exhaled.

He took the pipe from my outstretched hand and smiled. "I have all the time in the world."

Ever conscientious after a hit, he capped it with the flat side of our Bic to put it out quickly, then placed the pipe down on the table. He pulled a Marlboro from the pack next to it. Tobacco lit; he turned toward the highway. The lights of the semis speared the darkness. Through a billow of smoke, he frowned, his brow tightened and bunched. "I'm no mahatma, but it seems to me that the Earth we live on is a delicate unity of vast, intricate proportions."

Concentrated and tense about my next move, I nodded with vague interest. "Dude, where the hell did that come from?"

He shrugged. "Just letting my mind wander."

"Well, let it wander back to the game, okay?"

Part of me felt indignant at his casual demeanor toward our match. Indignant because he should've been focused like me. But admittedly, I was also indignant with myself because he was so much better than me and he didn't need to concentrate on our moves.

But he continued, seemingly oblivious to my tone or glare. "And when they're disrupted, we suffer. And we've been doing a lot disrupting throughout our so-called development as a species and civilization. Doesn't it seem like complete and utter folly that we don't spend enough time getting in touch with and nurturing the harmony that's all around us?"

"I guess. Maybe. Pay attention to the game, Jack."

He turned back to me. "Since we're dependent upon this planet, I think being humble before it would do us a world of good."

I chuckled. "Jack."

"I think we're conceited—"

With a trepidatious hand, I slid my king one square. "Jack."

"and arrogant thinking that we're so civilized, so advanced, so smart when in actuality we're not very emotionally mature."

I leaned back a bit, my hands resting on my knees. "Dude, the game."

He took another drag, then dropped the cigarette in the quarter-full water bottle.

Pfsssh.

"We're overlooking the obvious," he stated.

Indignance turned into impatience. "The *game*, Jack."

"That finding more of a balance, some harmony would ground us with this world, and do more to advance us than any religion, or science, ever could." He paused. "That's where I'd like to spend my time, my energy. But so far, sadly, pathetically, I've never been able to come close to achieving that."

After another hit, his chin rested on the cupped palm of his left hand. He passed the pipe and, without a moment of doubt, his right hand surely moved his rook along the edge of the board into the last row of my territory. He looked up with bland interest. "Checkmate."

I leaned forward and scowled at the chess board. "Oh, what the fuck." I took a hit and scratched my head.

After another in a seemingly endless string of bruising losses, a series of beatings, my chess ego, meagre that it had been, was crushed.

"I'm done," I said with a sigh.

I only beat him once.

I suspect he may have let me.

Stay

The sun is rising over the Drury Inn in Denver.

'How do you feel like you've failed me?' Jack asks from the silken, plush armchair.

Three steps and I flop down into the adjoining chair. A sip of my coffee, swiveling my head to look at my friend. *'Because I couldn't help you when you needed it the most. Now, you're gone. And I don't want you to be gone, Jack. Can you understand that?'*

He looks out the window. I can tell he's contemplating my words, his brow furrowing in thought like it always does. Lips frowning while he ponders the best way to state his feelings. *'Do you feel that if I'm not physically here anymore, then your own life, the life we had together, won't be real?'*

'Yeah. I'm afraid of that.'

'Well, I don't have to go anywhere. I can stay here for as long as you like. That's up to you now.' A pause. *'Hey, guess what? Today you'll get to talk to my sister.'*

'Do you think that will help?'

'Undoubtedly.'

The shadows are shortening on the slopes of the mountains.

It's almost time.

'I gotta go soon,' I say.

'I know. But I'll be with you.'

Hauling my ass out of the chair, I slug down the rest of my coffee, toss the empty, bleached paper cup with its polyethylene lining into the trash, and snatch the TV remote off the bed where it's tangled in the sheets from the night before. Finding The Weather Channel, I listen to the morning banter while gathering my toiletries.

Warm sunshine with a few scattered clouds, but watch out for those thunderstorms which may be forming.

A hot shower and a lathery bar of soap. Brushed teeth and a quick swipe of fingers through hair. A fresh change of clothes—jeans, my faded "I put ketchup on my ketchup" T-shirt, and my battered Chuckies. Looking up, just below the ceiling, about eight feet high and out of reach, I notice an emergency sprinkler head attached to the wall.

A small sign is nailed next to it:

DO NOT HANG ITEMS FROM SPRINKLER HEAD

A bit of laughter to relieve my anxiety.

Who does that?

Food for Thought

"Ah, there it is. Our lodging for the night."

Somewhere near Great Basin in Nevada, he tugged on the reins of the Mustang and pulled into the gravel driveway of a campground.

Forty-five minutes later, we were checked in by the owner, a kindly, gnarled-faced old man dressed in a white checkered flannel shirt and faded blue jeans that looked to be two sizes too big for him, held up with a cracked leather belt. His hair was thick, full, and pearl white, immaculately combed and slicked back with oil. Perhaps Dapper Dan. He had a soft-spoken voice, blasé with an almost indetectable twang; the kind of voice that came with slow living out in the boonies. The tempo of unconcerned time.

Thrusting out our receipt with his liver spotted hand, he winked, then pulled a cigarillo from a pack of Davidoff that was tucked in his breast pocket. A Zippo came from nowhere. Quick as lightning, it rolled back and forth on his jeans and was lit. A high, bright flame illuminated the deep creases in his face, and the twinkle in his dark brown eyes. "You boys keep an ear out for coyotes, ya hear?"

Jack and I looked at each other. Both of us read each other's minds as we tried not to laugh.

Jack nodded once. "Oh, we will, sir. You can bet your boots on that."

The man looked slowly down, then up, and digested the comment.

"Ain't got my boots on." A billow of smoke settled around his oiled hair.

All eyes flickered over each other, then I spoke. "Thank you. We'll be fine. We have experience with these things."

The man puffed on his cigarillo. "Well, don't go bettin' your Keds on that, sonny. The coyotes will run ya 'till your feet smoke."

"Thanks. We appreciate it."

The man smiled. "I'll be closin' up soon. If you need some vittles, poke around over there." He fluttered his hand toward the other side of the one room, to a plank wood lobby where the small general store was. "Got some of my homemade elk sausage on ice over there in the cooler, if that suits your fancy."

"You make your own sausage?" venerated Jack, with an air of incredulity.

"Ain't that what I just said?" The man shook his head. "Nippers. They never listen."

"Do you have any hot ones?" Jack asked. He turned with eagerness and headed toward the far wall, toward the chest nestled in the corner.

"Hot *and* sweet. I'll wait for ya. Then, I'm goin' in the back. It's where I catch my reruns of Family Feud and I Love Lucy." Another puff. "Love that Lucy. She's a hoot. A good looker too. And that Dawson gets to kiss all the ladies." He winked again. "Lucky devil."

"We won't be long," I said, as I followed Jack and began to look for buns.

○

Soon after, camp was established.

A light, cool breeze touched our hair and whispered through the junipers, Ponderosa pines, and Englemann spruce as we sat by the fire listening to the crackle of the flames and watching the sparks rise. Above and beyond, there was nothing but the eternal voice of emptiness that communed with the darkness. Dreamily, I watched Jack as he pierced the end of yet another sausage with a sharpened tree branch.

Snap.

Hiss.

"Sure beats a gas station sandwich, doesn't it," he proclaimed. He leaned forward and peeked into the anodized aluminum saucepan perched between two rocks next to the fire. "Beans are almost hot."

"I'll get some in a minute," I said, slightly distracted. My sight was absorbed by the orange, shimmering coals that we had built in a mound under the fresh branches. A purified shimmer, soon to be ash and absorbed back into the Earth for nourishment.

For life.

Ashes to ashes, dust to dust.

Jack shifted to the ground, leaning back on his rock. His sausage was cooked—charred—the way he liked it. And with a smooth, practiced motion, he slid it from the end of the branch into a bun. His hand squeezed around it. "This is where it's at. Quiet, away from the fears of so-called civilization. I don't need or want or fear much out here, away from everything. Coyotes. Bears. Wolves. Why be afraid? They're nothing when you compare them with living among our own species."

I nodded and took a sip of beer—Rolling Rock, at Jack's insistence.

The flames leaped; the wood crackled. Small embers drifted up into the sky. Jack took a fearsome bite of his sausage, half of it at once.

Voracious as always.

"Fear is a funny thing," he chewed. "It's the root cause of most of our problems and confronting it, overcoming it, is something most of us don't do. Most people live in a sort of quiet desperation. That causes needs that can be emotionally unhealthy. And lasting happiness will never be achieved if you live like that. You don't have to look very far in America, around at our species, to see it."

I could tell he was in one of his philosophical moods. And as always, I did my best to participate and contribute.

"I can understand that."

He poked at the fire. More sparks and embers floated through the air. "A lot of people gravitate toward momentary happiness, not true happiness. And maybe that's because they're afraid to, or can't, look inside themselves honestly. I think the most likely cause is that our society mainly promotes momentary happiness through materialism or superficiality. By that I mean, getting a Starbucks Latte or a new DVD or a new car or a new couch. For that matter, eating these sausages and beans tonight is a momentary happiness. It makes you feel good at the moment. But it doesn't provide for a lasting internal joy."

I nodded as he slid another sausage onto his branch and thrust it into the flames. "It's kinda like people are always moving from one orgasm to another, isn't it?" I mused. "One materialistic fling after another."

He chuckled and turned his sausage, a brief flame shooting up from it as the grease caught. "Yeah, we've had a love affair with materialism for a long time. But if our existence is solely based on momentary tidbits of commerce and consumerism, then the soul inevitably becomes bankrupt of what it really means to be human."

I thought for a moment and took a sip of beer. Something had begun to rise to the surface of my mind. Hard to articulate, as if seen through a veil. There, but not there. "Here's a thought. Do you suppose that the actual act of eating provides a momentary joy, but the act of sharing food together provides the lasting joy you're talking about?"

He looked at me and smiled. "I'm glad you understand, Dana. And that you've tolerated me all these years. All my trite nonsense.

I find it hard to share these thoughts with people. Mostly, they look at me like I'm an alien."

"Just don't shoot me with your laser gun, buddy." I smiled. "But tolerating you has nothing to do with it. You're my best friend, Jack. Besides, I think our talks are cool. They help me. And I really love our times like this. When we're on the road, just hangin' out." I took another sip of my beer, grabbed the stick we had chosen for the fire, and poked at the flames. "What would I do without you showing me how to see things differently?"

We gazed into each other's eyes for a moment.

Another sausage charred and slid into a bun. "Me too. But so yeah, to come back to it. Without a doubt, you're on to something. And on a personal note, a long-lasting relationship, an intimate one formed from years of hard work, is typically what provides the best internal contentment. Another example of what I'm talking about. My parents never had that. Neither did yours."

"How do you find it, Jack?"

He looked perturbed. Vexed at something within him. He shook his head. "I'm not sure yet, but I've always wanted to form something better than what they did, so I can actually look in the mirror and like what I see."

"Are you okay?" I asked.

He nodded "Yeah. Have some beans, and I'll keep working on finding my better half."

The flames leaped and small embers floated.

They rose to the sky.

Elusive.

Reunion Drive

After talking to Libby on the phone and riding the silken voice of the Drury Inn's elevator again, the once soothing pleasant, female, robotic courtesy voice now reflecting my own tight-shouldered edginess back to me—

"Going down."

"Yeah, I know you are," I wink.

Swish.

Clump, whir, clump.

Another monotonal *ding.*

Swish.

"First floor."

"You're the boss."

I'm soon in front of the hotel, waiting on the sidewalk under the bright, smog filtered sun. The massive hulk of the Front Range—the Blue and Crescent Mountains, along with Centralia—is beginning to fade somewhat with the haze of Denver's daily activities. Mount Tom is there too, just west of where Jack shot himself.

The slopes of White Ranch Park.

Across the lot, I catch Libby's old, dented, forest green 2001 Subaru Forester swinging in. Winding its way through the maze of cars—Florida, Washington, California, New Jersey, Maine, Vermont, and Michigan.

A wide, happy grin greets me through the windshield as she slows to a stop, the brakes squealing, the engine ticking over. The smile I return is filled with warmth as the passenger window slides down. I'm happy not only because it's been years since we've seen each other, but there's never been animosity between us.

But also because I'm nervous. I'm still trepidatious about this memorial; at how I might feel. And how reality will smack me in the head. I'm heavy. Somber. Even slightly gloomy because this physical event makes mortality undeniable. A fortiori that within my heart must dwell incomprehensible grief.

I hope I can face this.

But I'm also smiling because, during our phone call, we had agreed to go to the memorial together—both for me not knowing where it was going to be held and for a sense of mutual security. A reciprocal aura of comfort at having each other's back. To ease any awkwardness that might arise. From seeing people from both our pasts, and Jack's, from whom we might want to escape.

There's always someone at these events who brings up unpleasant memories.

The standard, "I remember when..." or "The last time I saw you we fought about..." or "You're drinking more than I remember..."

Or escape that might even come in the form of just plain having enough. Enough of catching up. Enough of somber faces. Enough of speculation and reminiscence and emotion.

We decided to be reluctant buddies on the front lines of bereavement.

And there's something extraordinary and particular about re-connecting with someone you haven't seen in a long time. Sitting here now, in the passenger seat, I'm overcome with the sensation; the marvel everyone must feel at a reunion.

She's changed. And so, have I.

I look her up and down, taking in her black tank top with lacy strings. Her olive drab canvas pants. Her sleeve tattoo of a Griffin, its claws clutching a bouquet of lavender. Her graceful shoulders and elegant neck. Firm, strong jawline and high cheek bones. Smooth, tanned skin and ample, round breasts. My mind acknowledges that she's here; that we're really sitting next to each other.

"You changed your hair. What made you go blonde?"

"I got tired of the red."

"I like it, and you look great," I say. "You haven't changed a bit."

"That's what everyone says when they meet up."

"Yeah, but I mean it. No polite bullshit. You really do look fantastic."

"Thanks. So do you. But I have. I'm edging on fifty now and I'm fatter. Too much of the good life, I suppose."

"People say that too. But I don't think so."

She smiles. "Trust me, I have. My ass has gotten big."

"I'll have to check it out when we get to the restaurant."

"Don't bother."

"But I want to. I'll give you my honest opinion."

She laughs. "You're too kind."

But even though meeting her feels somewhat awkward, even clumsy at first, like learning how to drive a standard shift car, once talking, our conversation begins flowing like smooth gears shifting. As if it was just yesterday when our eyes met. When our arms embraced and auras mixed. When our thoughts were expressed. Our feelings and experiences related. Shared and bonded. And I feel an odd sense of appreciation, like the sun on my face after a long, gloomy day.

But some things haven't changed.

She still weaves through traffic with untroubling ease, feet smoothly pumping pedals while up and downshifting. The occasional grimace when someone cuts her off. I can see her temptation to honk; it's written all over her face as she lowers her chin, eyes steadily boring into the Lincoln Navigator in front of us at a stop light. The light turns green and we're all on our way. A quick flick of a signal. A change of lanes. Polished as glass city driving.

Jack was the same way. Only a lot of the time, I felt tense with him. Sometimes he even scared me, although I never recognized the feeling until later. A delayed awareness that rose to the surface of my consciousness when the distraction of the drive was over.

And it was always in the city, where there was a congestion of people. Out on the deserted miles of roadway, traveling on a new adventure, he was typically calm. Even happy. It's only now that I'm marking the difference with his demeanor.

But Libby's never made me feel tense. She always seemed much calmer no matter where she was. Relaxed. Matter of fact and deferential. She's a part of the thoroughfares, avenues, and boulevards. The skyscrapers, churches, and businesses. The people and the hum of hustle and bustle. To her, it's just another day in the gridlock.

Not Jack. Jack seemed angry somehow. More aggressive in a pernicious way, as if the streets belonged to him and no one else. He claimed the lights, the signs, and the pavement without anyone's knowledge.

Anti-social within the confines of his car cocoon.

And you had better get out of the way.

Bully

I shifted as the school bus jostled over a small bump in the road, and the metal support brace dug into my back. But I was deeply uncomfortable for more reasons than the steel, and the stiff, worn padding. I was hemmed in by four kids who leaned over the torn, brown, pleather seats, behind and in front of me. The four kids who made me desperately wish I was invisible.

Their faces leered down at me. Their voices surrounded me. Their fingers jabbed at me through the air. Their eyes glowed with fiery exaltation, scorching my rapid, frightened heart which pounded against my rib cage. All daggers that shrunk my eleven-year-old body further into the cushion.

And I was abandoned as Jack sat sideways in the seat across the aisle. So close. So far away as he ignored the plea of my eyes. As he laughed and joined in, callous to my fear.

"He looks like Q*bert with that nose, doesn't he?" Jack asked the other three boys.

"Yeah, and look at how small his hands are," chided one of them.

"Kinda puny," agreed another.

"The only thing worse is having a small dick," proposed another.

"Well, with a nose like that, I bet he does," concluded the first boy.

"But it would make a good place for birds to perch," mused Jack.

"I bet when he sneezes everyone runs for cover," chortled the second boy.

"*I* bet if he gets a boner and walks into a wall, his nose will break first," pondered another.

"If it was any bigger, it'd be a foot," criticized the third.

"Yeah, and who mows your nose hair, big nose?" chided the first again.

Defenseless and forsaken, I turned toward the window and the bright, late spring sunshine that poured over my flushed face. Tears leaked down my cheeks, my lips trembling with the sting of resentment; of swollen anger.

"Aww, look, he's crying," exclaimed Jack.

"Don't make him cry," yelled one of the boys. "He'll flood the bus with snot"

Jack burst into laughter, then said, his face suddenly deadpan as his blue/gray eyes bored into me with a malevolence I hadn't experienced before, "You know, somewhere there's a tree that's working really hard to make oxygen for you. You should apologize to it."

Claustrophobic to the point of panic, I wished that I could've opened the window and jumped out. But all I could do was sit there.

"What ya gonna do, big nose?" scolded one of the boys.

I tried to ignore them.

Why was he doing this to me? Why had he turned on me, joined with the other kids and picked on me? I didn't understand anything except that for the first time I could think of, I hated him.

"He's not going to do anything," stated Jack, flat and monotone. "You know why? 'Cause he's a wimp. A retard and a wimp."

Before I knew what happened, the words poured from my lips. "Oh Yeah? Well, your dad likes Chris better. I bet he wishes you were never born."

I was desperate for him to stop. I knew it would make him hurt. A nearly equal exchange of injury because he knew I was profoundly self-conscious about my looks.

His face became expressionless. Dead. Gone somewhere else. He broke eye contact, turned away, and rested his arms on top of the adjoining seat. Slow and steady, his finger tapped the top of the cushion.

Silent.

Without a word, he got off the bus. And I followed. It seemed as if he did not have a care in the world. Oblivious to my very presence as he sauntered down the steps, out onto the grassy embankment, then down the road toward his house.

I didn't intend to fight my best friend when I woke up that day. When we parted ways for our first morning class at school. When we met for lunch in the cafeteria. Or when we got on the bus for the ride home. I didn't want to hurt him, but I also couldn't understand why he had turned on me; not come to my side.

I ran to catch up. "Hey," I yelled.

He stopped, turned, and asked, "What?"

"How could you?"

"How could I what?"

"You don't know?"

He cocked his head with vague curiosity. "No, not really. Why don't you just leave me alone."

I lunged and pushed him with all my might. He barely budged. He looked at me for a moment with those dead eyes. Then, with two steps, he was on me.

"I'm going to rip your head off and shit down your neck," he screamed.

I pushed back and he screamed again. No words this time, just a shriek that seemed to come from the very depths of his body. A scream that was hideously high-pitched and filled with blind fury.

His fists clenched and unclenched. His face burned a dark red, swollen with fury. A twitch that contorted his lips into a snarl. He tackled me and, before I knew it, we were rolling on the ground, sweaty arms wantonly swatting at each other, dirt and grass stuck to our clothes. By the fourth or fifth roll, he straddled me.

His knees squashed my elbows into the ground, and tingles ran through them. His hands pressed against my shoulders, and I could feel their bruise. I felt a rock jut into my lower back. The sun blinded me as I looked up, his face absurdly framed by the wide-open, bright blue sky. His spittle doused my face as he screamed again. And I laid there, by this time all my angry energy drained.

Now more shocked than anything else.

Without another utterance, he stood and looked at me, a bland, almost sedated contemplation on his face. "Don't you ever talk about my father again," he said. Then, as if nothing had happened, he gathered his schoolbooks that were sprayed in the grass around us, turned, and walked away.

I don't remember how long I lay in the grass and looked up at the sky; a sky with popcorn clouds that drifted lazily on the unseen, indifferent air currents. I don't know how long I waited for the thud of disbelief to clear from my head. The fear to dissipate from my heart, and the hammer of bewilderment to stop pounding my mind.

Eventually, I climbed to my feet.

Libby and the Long Talk

The Yak and Yeti.

I look out the window as Libby swings into the parking lot, curious to see this new restaurant. I'm half expecting to see something resembling a Sasquatch Museum from the California mountains—a display case of plaster cast footprints, a twenty-foot statue of a menacing, shaggy man/gorilla, and bags of hair samples for sale. So I'm surprised when I see the simple, plain exterior; and a little charmed by the yellow, stucco walls. The flat roof with a corrugated, red metal awning. The large, rectangular windows with flat red trim. The wooden, two-rail fence with flaking red paint surrounding the unassuming shrubbery among a few young trees.

My stomach growls and, several minutes later, Libby and I are across from each other in a brown, pleather booth at a laminated wood table. We've ordered from a lovely, young Indian girl who spoke so fast and with such a thick accent behind her Covid mask that I could barely understand her. I could see Libby smirking out of the corner of my eye. She's having the Chana Masala and I'm looking forward to trying the Lamb Kadai. We're sharing the garlic na'an.

She takes a sip of her Masala Chai tea, both of us wondering how to begin the heavier side of the conversation.

"So how are you? Are you doing okay with all of this?"

Her eyes wander to the window next to us, to the bright sunshine glinting off the cars in the half-full parking lot and a small Canyon Maple shivering in the light breeze. Her fingers are pulling on the string of the tea bag, slowly dipping it up and down. "I am. I mean, don't get me wrong. I've had my – moments." She looks back at me. "I've been crying a lot, often when I don't expect it, when I'm painting or sitting in traffic or making coffee in the morning. But I've slowly gotten used to not feeling his presence; gotten used to the idea that he's really gone. Sometimes, I've wondered if I'm sad for me or sadder for him."

"What do you mean?" I ask.

"That he felt so truly hopeless that he felt he had to do it, that there was nothing else he could've done." She pauses and takes a deep breath. "Wow, that all came out one big gush. Sorry."

I'm not in the least offended. Listening to her reminds me of some of the rants I would spill out after the war. Only mine were full of rage, violence, and for the most part, uncontrolled. "It's okay. No worries. Sounds like it needed to."

Her shoulders slump. "It did." Then she launches in again. "Do you think that's denigrating?"

"You mean, like having pity; looking down on him in some way?"

"Yes."

I ponder for a moment. "No, I don't think so. And I understand what you're talking about; about feeling his presence. Would you think I'm crazy if I told you he's with me; that we talk, that when I ask questions, he answers me?"

"I don't think that's crazy at all. It's your mind trying to come to grips with it, that's all." She takes a sip of tea. "Besides, I believe in the spirit world. I often like to think that he's merged with the universe, that his energy is with everything now. Just because he no longer exists physically, he still exists. He's pure energy. That which we all loved is still here and we can still connect with him if we choose."

"So, I'm not a whackjob?"

"Not in the least."

I relax back on my seat. "He loved you very much, Libby. You know that, right?"

"I know he did. And he loved you too."

"I think he really loved the time you two were together."

"Well, it wasn't always roses, especially toward the end."

"Yeah, so what happened anyway? You know I pretty much dropped out after the war. I'm so very sorry for that, I really am. It was such a dark time in my life, and I was totally out of my head."

"You don't need to apologize. I can't begin to imagine." Another sip of tea. "I remember many nights worrying about you. Jack worried too. You seemed to be far away somehow, in another space, some sort of ether we couldn't reach."

"I was. I think the only shred of salvation I managed to pull out of it, at the time anyway, was that I filed for conscientious objector."

"And that went through?"

I nod. "I was discharged under that status. It was a win for my soul."

"I'm glad."

"And writing about it helped too. Writing can be very therapeutic; cathartic in the sense of processing."

"I can appreciate that. My art is the same way. It helps me deal. Have you published lately?"

I grin, a smirk born from a combination of happiness, pride, and weariness. Exhaustion akin to a marathon runner after crossing an invisible finish line. Elated and fortunate, but with a finale that never truly exists. "Despite everything, yes. I managed to put out that second book. I squeezed it in wherever I could," I add.

"Well, I'll have to read it."

"I hope you do."

Our food arrives. Copper/stainless steel Handis. Steam gently rising from the deep, creamy colors of the sauces. A Thali with piled, golden brown na'an. Aromatic rice with a cilantro garnish. A stainless-steel carousel of chutneys—Tamarind, Mint Cilantro, and Chili Garlic.

"Would you like some more tea or water?" asks our server.

A moment's hesitation, my mind ticking through her accent. "I'd love some more lemon water."

"Of course. Anything else?"

I look at Libby. Libby looks at me, then she says, "No, this all looks fantastic. Thank you so much."

"I'll be back with your water." The young woman disappears through a door to the kitchen.

While piling our plates, Libby smiles, "Jack and I were happy for a long, long time, you know that, right?" Her voice seems wistful as she begins reliving her life with Jack. A part of her still there, she's almost meditative, as if, even after all this time, she's still smoothing out the wrinkles of how everything transpired. I'm sure it tugs at her heart underneath the thin, poker-faced veil she's wearing.

"I do."

"I think it truly began when we bought the house, the one on High Street."

"I remember it well. I have a lot of good memories there, particularly after I came home. It was a refuge for me in a lot of ways."

"We wanted it to be. We really wanted to care for you."

"I know."

"Anyway, looking back on it, we really began falling apart in that insidious, very typical way a lot of couples do. You know, slowly at first, barely perceptible, but mounting all the time until it's just square in your face one day."

I nod. "I'm familiar with that. I think Rita and I were like that."

My water arrives and I squeeze the lemon wedge into it. Taking a sip, I'm struck by the contrast of how tart and refreshing it is. Like a relationship can be. Or the end of one that's taken a wrong turn.

"We were pretty happy at first, and preoccupied with settling in, decorating – and with Jack finding a new job."

"The one with the forest service."

"Yeah. The one that he really wanted. At that point, he was ready to move on from being a paramedic. Not that he didn't like it, he did, but I think he really wanted to be outside more, you know, in the wilderness, where I think his heart really belonged."

"That sounds like him. And I remember that. He was still a hotshot when I was overseas."

"Right. And I was always entirely supportive of him doing it." She spoons more Masala and rice onto her plate, then takes another slice of na'an. "But neither of us realized just how much he would be gone. It wasn't just the summer. Sometimes the fire season extended well into autumn and when there weren't any fires, there was always something for him to do that kept him away."

"Trucking life is rough like that too. Always gone. It's hell on having a family."

"I know. My stepfather was a trucker. But I began to want one – a family, that is. I really wanted to settle in. Maybe it's the Midwesterner in me, or that I had a not-so-great family, but I've always wanted that solid," she laughs, "boring, stay-at-home family life. Something stable, you know?"

"I do. But I know now that I've never really been cut out for that. My wanderlust is too strong."

"Yeah, well, his was too. And it was maybe a year or so into that job that even when he was home during the off-season, he spent most of his time drinking and playing around with his SUVs. He was restless. Irritable. I think we fell into a rut. I think he just got bored with me."

"Did you guys ever talk about having a family?"

"Oh sure. I brought it up. And he would actively participate in our conversation. He seemed very interested and enthusiastic, but after a while I began to think that he was humoring me more than anything. Well, maybe that's not quite right. He was," while clutching her fork, her fingers making air quotes, "pretending to be interested, like he thought, 'This is what I'm supposed to be doing in life,' only his heart wasn't in it; he wasn't really interested."

"Like he was doing a duty, right? Some sort of duty that he felt a pressure to do?"

"Yeah. Exactly. But the pressure wasn't just from me. We were in our thirties. It was what we were supposed to be doing."

"Sounds like he was trying to convince himself, more than anything else."

"I think so too. He never got angry or was mean about it. I could just tell that even when we were talking, half of him was somewhere else, like on the road or something. And I think, as he felt more pressure to settle down, his drinking and absenteeism went up. He also felt more and more emotionally absent."

"He was escaping."

"Yes. And he lost interest in me. It was as if he didn't see me. Even favors were becoming a hassle for me to ask for. Like I was always vexing him with tidbits that he just couldn't be bothered with. I began to feel very lonely. I think both of us were lonely, even when we were together."

"Like ghosts."

"Yeah, like ghosts just passing each other in the house, tied down with responsibilities. Nothing more."

Finished with her Masala, only a few stray grains of rice remaining, she nibbles a last bite of na'an. "I think that he just didn't want to grow up. That little boy adventurer in him was too strong and wouldn't loosen the grip of what he felt was freedom. It got unbearable, so, in the end, I just told him one day that I couldn't do it anymore and was planning on moving out."

"How did he take it?"

"Good, actually. Although it felt hurtful. He was so matter of fact, so aloof. I almost wish he 'd have gotten angry – or I don't know – anything."

"Like it would've meant more to him?"

"Yeah. At least I would've known there was still some passion for us inside him."

"Did you guys keep in touch a lot?"

"Oh sure. We didn't hate each other. We agreed to be friends, and we sold the house. He found a place downtown and I moved out here. It worked out okay and, in some ways, I think we were better friends in the end."

"I'm sorry. He didn't talk about it with me."

"He probably didn't talk about it with anyone. That wasn't his style. But one thing happened about a year after that threw me."

I push away my empty plate and sit back. "What was that?"

"He called me out of the blue one day and wanted to get together; go for a bike ride or take a walk."

"And did you?"

"Sure. Why not? Like I told you, we were still fine as friends. So, we got together, took a great ride up into the mountains and he took me to this spot that he liked out in White Ranch."

This startles me. I'm sure we both know the significance of that spot. But neither of us mentions it.

Crack.

The shot echoes in my head.

"We sat down, just watching the scenery, enjoying the sun, and he launched into a huge talk about our relationship. He asked me all sorts of questions. I think he was trying to figure out what went wrong between us. Things like, 'How was I not good enough?' 'What ways do you think I could've done better?' 'What do you think was the root cause for us failing?' That sort of thing."

"That sounds like his usual analytical mind trying to sort it out."

"But what really hit me was when he said, 'You know, I still love you. I might be open to trying again, you know.'"

"Jack always approached relationships in a very practical way."

"I know."

"It was something that we never really agreed on. But it sounds like he was trying to get beyond that somehow." I think for a moment. "It sounds like he was really trying to reach out, but he didn't know how. What did you say?"

"I didn't know what to say, other than I had already moved on. I really didn't want to get involved with us again. I felt it was over."

She falls silent. The restaurant is silent as well. We're the only ones left, the lunch hour over. I take a sip of water, her story churning in my mind.

Then something occurs to me. "Do you feel that…" I'm trying to find the right words, "that this was his way of maybe – in some sort of passive way, in his awkward way, of saying that he wanted to get back together? Only he wanted, maybe was waiting, for you to make the real, first move on that?"

She thinks for a moment, her brow furrowing. "Perhaps. At the time, it didn't occur to me like that. It wasn't long after, that he met Saige."

"Do you know that I've never even met her?"

"I have, but only once. Did he want you to?"

"Well, we did drift apart for a while after I got home. It's something I regret." I look down at the table, swirling the water in my glass, the melting ice clinking softly.

"I'm sorry to hear that. He never talked about it with me."

"Never?"

"No. But that's not entirely surprising. He could be very closed like that. Sometimes it was very difficult to draw him out and get him to express his feelings."

My eyes wander to the large, wall painting of Yaks ponderously hauling supplies up a mountain ridge and the sculptures of Lord Ganesha, Mataji, and Shiva, then over the hand-knotted, richly patterned rugs and hard wood flooring, and finally under the Moroccan pendant lanterns. But they're not really looking at the decor.

"I know," I reply slowly, my mind not wanting to relive that time. "But regardless, it hurt. I needed him. And I remember reaching out and reaching out. After a while, I really felt like I put him out for some reason, like I was a bother."

My stomach bubbles with unease.

"I'm sure that wasn't the case. He loved you very much, Dana."

"I hope so. In any case, we met up in Vermont in 2015 at a friend's pseudo high school reunion and we just started right up like no time was lost – like nothing had ever happened. But he never mentioned Saige, his marriage, the kids. Nothing. It was more our usual, fun banter and him wanting to know all about what I'd been doing. I told him about writing my first book and publishing it. And that I was thinking of going to grad school. All that jazz." I laugh now, the bubble of pain dispersing. The fondness of the memory taking me. "He told me I'd be an asshole not to do it, considering I had my G.I. Bill. He was actually the final impetus for me making the decision. My affirming inspiration, so to speak. Leave it to Jack."

"I'm glad you guys had that time together."

"Well, it was a beginning – a new beginning. We were back in touch after that, and I thought we had all the time we wanted or needed. So, what do you know about this Saige?"

"I don't know a whole lot. I think they met online; one of those dating websites. Jack was tightlipped about her."

"Is she going to be at the memorial? I'd like to meet her."

"From what Avery told me, no. She decided that it would be

best not to be there for some reason. Avery didn't elaborate, and I felt it best not to pry."

This all feels very mysterious to me. I feel my mind trying to sort everything out, like an ill-equipped Sherlock Holmes, floundering in the shadows with a cracked magnifying glass.

"Did you go to the wedding?"

"No," she states.

"But you got an invite?"

"I did."

"Why didn't you go?"

"I don't know, exactly. Only that I felt uncomfortable about it."

"I got a standard invite in the mail. As a guest. Not even a phone call. And I gotta be honest, I thought it was hurtful. I mean, Jesus, he was my best man. You would think I would be some part of the wedding party. An usher maybe." I pause. "I ended up not going, either. And it's something I regret now." I sigh. "Do you think he was upset with us for not going?"

"If he was, he never said anything."

"Me neither. What else do you know about Saige?"

"Well, Jack did call me from time to time. He told me that they were happy together, that he had found his better half, and that she was the love of his life."

"Did he seem happy? Like, really happy? Or was he faking it?"

"If I had to guess, I think he was happy – at first. Maybe it was the honeymoon phase. I don't know. But he did seem to settle, which made me a little angry since it was such a problem when we were together too. They moved into her house. She had already owned it when they met."

"Maybe he was looking for shelter. You know?"

"That could have been the case. Absolutely. I know that he was jobless for a while, wondering what to do with himself. He had to leave the forest service because of all the steel in his body. He couldn't take it anymore; his hip was really beginning to bother him. So, he was looking for a new adventure, one that was a little easier on him. He found a state job."

"He did mention that at the reunion. I thought it was odd, him working in an office. I've never been able to picture him there."

"I thought it was odd too. It was in the accounting office. They're responsible for accounts receivable and payable, employee services, payroll, Eco Pass bills – that sort of thing. But he seemed resigned, almost as if he was shrugging his shoulders at it all. And I remember him calling shortly after. He wanted to go back to college and get an economics degree."

"Makes sense, given how he liked to analyze everything. But I could see him getting into economics as a hobby, not as a career."

She shrugs. "Anyway, I think he was content for a while. But as time went on, he sounded more and more melancholy on the phone when he would call. And I started to worry. He sounded lifeless. There wasn't the usual happy-go-lucky spark to it. The only time it rebounded was when he told me him and Saige had decided to have a family and that she was pregnant."

I sit back in my seat clutching my water glass. I take a long sip from it. "Now that is something I never could and can come to grips with. I just can't see him as a father. Not that he would be an asshole or anything. It's just – I don't know how to put it."

"He wouldn't want the responsibility?" she suggests.

"Yeah."

"I understand. I felt the same way. But you know, we met up after the first was born. Jack and I took a walk together one afternoon. Just one of those city park walks. Such an adorable little kid. And he was good with him. Really. Very comfortable. Very loving. He seemed to really go full throttle into it. Although I couldn't help but laugh a little. Here he was, with a baby in a stroller. It felt so comically opposite from the man I knew."

I smile. "Sounds like something out of a bad rom com."

She looks at her watch. "We should probably go. The memorial started about an hour ago. Like I said, it's supposed to be casual, at a bar, but—"

"A bar?"

"Yep."

An ironic smile burgeons across my face. "That figures."

As I follow her out of the restaurant, I can't help but glance down. She has a nice ass. Then I sigh. The moment is here; the one thing I really don't want to do. And I'm left with more questions.

Always more questions.

Somewhere, Anywhere

'Been quite the day, hasn't it?'

I sigh. *'It has.'*

Through the windows of the Drury Inn, the stars have begun their dusk till dawn overlook as the sun slips behind the mountains—a leftover, brilliant orange spread across the ridgeline. Blending with a luster of deep purple.

'I thought the memorial was interesting,' says Jack from the silken, plush armchair.

'Interesting is one word for it. Not what I expected.'

He shrugs. *'It was a memorial. What did you think was going to happen?'*

'I don't know. Something. You know, anything. Answers, I guess. I mean, all it was, was a little get together in a bar with some drinks and quesadillas. Bad quesadillas at that.' I see Jack grimace out of the corner of my eye. *'But overall, for me, it just felt hollow somehow. I think the only thing I'm glad about is that Avery pulled me aside so we could set up our talk; just the two of us.'*

He smiles. *'I think you had a preformed vision of what memorials are supposed to be, Dana.'*

I let my head flop back onto the cushion of my own silken, plush armchair and look at Jack. *'You're probably right about that.'* I turn back to the watchful stars, close my eyes, and sigh. *'I have a confession to make, Jack.'*

'What's that?'

'It feels weird to be here.'

'You mean in Denver?'

'Yeah, but I mean here, on the fifth floor.'

'Why?'

'Because for some reason it feels contrary to what I would call soul searching; of where I need to be so I can unravel a lifetime spent with you.'

'Where would you rather be?'

My finger points to some vague, undefined spot out the window. *'Out there.'*

Jack shrugs. *'Nature's a wonderful venue, to be sure.'*

'That sounds about right.'

'But it does beg the question, Dana. Does it really matter what space you're in to wrestle with important questions?'

'Doesn't it?'

'Not really. Call it what you will. Soul searching. A vision quest. How about an examination of conscience, or some sort of shamanic journey? Whatever. Regardless of the term, it's an inward experience. Location is irrelevant because everything on Earth has energy. Concrete buildings or a Redwood. Grass or AstroTurf. It's all one in the same.'

'If that's true, Jack, then everything is nature—'

'Right.'

'and I should be able to sort everything out no matter where I happen to plant, pardon the pun, myself.'

'Or even when you're driving. It's just preference, Dana. Nothing more.'

I sigh again. *'I don't know if I can do that. It feels easier said, then done, Jack.'*

'You struggle with these things because of the American myth that says you need to travel somewhere to discover yourself. To go somewhere, anywhere, to the west for instance, to find your answers, and thereby happiness. Maybe even some peace.' He looks at me with a wry grin.

'You moved to Denver, then Montana. You've moved here and there, even joined the army, with the notion that somewhere beyond a horizon your answers would be found; hoping that over there must be better than over here. And I think it's obvious you haven't gotten what you needed.'

I chuckle. *'That sounds about right. But Jack, you didn't find happiness either.'*

'No, no, I didn't, even though I certainly tried in a lot of places – like that ledge we were sitting on outside of Moab.'

I frown and scratch my head. *'What am I missing, Jack?'*

Jack closes his eyes. *'I'm guessing, but I feel safe in doing so, that, like me, you've intellectualized these ideas but haven't taken the next step. Haven't allowed these ideas, as well as the emotions associated with them, to come to the surface in the way that they should. That you've held onto them, and me, with a pretty tight grip.'* He pauses, then, *'You're overlooking the notion that a lot of things aren't about what we're told they should be. And maybe this journey you're on is more about an inward unbecoming of everything you thought you were supposed to be; everything that isn't the original person who's been buried underneath all the clatter of movies, TV, books, advertisements, school, our parents and friends. You gotta go back to being the real you, Dana, because the real you already has the answers.'*

I feel somewhat shrunken. Drained because no matter how hard I try, I feel as if I always forget what I've learned. Life lessons that should be engrained by now. *'Actually, believe it or not, the war taught me that. I guess I forgot.'*

'That's normal. No one's immune from that. I spent years waxing pathetic on this concept.'

We're silent for a while, each of us gazing out over the darkened horizon, the city lights glowing embers.

My lips tremble with the tears welling up in my eyes.

'I gotta be honest, Jack. All I really know right now is that my heart is broken.' He's watching me, but doesn't say anything, so I take a deep

breath and continue, *'I feel like there's a hole in me; like something's missing that I can't repair because you're my best friend – and now you're gone.'*

We both turn back to the window, contemplating my words. Then, he looks over his shoulder. *'She should be here soon.'*

Jack Street

Thump, thump.

Pulling myself out of the chair and consciously strolling to the hotel room door in an effort to relax, I take a deep breath before opening it.

A small smile greets me.

"Hi Dana. Sorry I'm a little late. People lingered at the memorial, and I had to spend that time with them."

I smile back and we look at each other for a moment. This is the first time we've had an opportunity to genuinely take each other in; to spend time together without distraction.

My eyes have to adjust.

Having had very little time with her during the memorial—she being lost to other's demands and me feeling incongruous while helplessly meandering like a ship without a rudder—I have to adjust to recognizing her as an adult. A grown woman, married with a career and children, and not the little girl I knew.

So many years.

Dressed in New Balance walking shoes, faded blue jeans, a loose ivory knit sweater, she's thin but with a healthy countenance. Shallow lines thread across her face in a few small places. Blonde hair drapes over her forehead. Not a gray to be seen. She looks good. And she's short. Petite enough to make her look somewhat comical with her purse and the large, white canvas tote slung over her shoulder. Both dwarf her.

Petite, but sturdy with resolve. Short, but tall in character.

A dignified and elegant presence.

But what strikes me the most is the intensity of her eyes. Blue/gray, like her brother's. They're discerning, collected, calm, yet sparkling with a life that looks right through another. Not cold and bland like her mother's; that calculated, critical gaze that had always made me uneasy.

"Oh, not a worry. It's all good. I was just hangin' out, eating my sub." I take a step back and sideways, sweeping my arm into the room. "Come on in. Welcome to my temporary, humble abode at the palatial accommodations of the Drury Inn."

I watch as she steps through the threshold.

"What's in the bag?" I ask.

She puts her purse, and the tote, down at the foot of my bed and turns. "Just some stuff that I felt you should have."

"Oh? Some of Jack's things?"

We sit face-to-face, each of us taking a bed. Without an answer, she instead drags the tote in front of her, rummaging through it, speaking softly with unwavering purposefulness. "First and foremost, I wanted to give you this."

She pulls out a round, clear Tupperware container with a red lid that's carefully sealed with packing tape. At first, I don't know what's inside. What could possibly be so important in a plastic container? But as she places it in my outstretched hand and I peer through the side, my breath catches and my thighs tense as the contents dawn on me.

I look at her and a wan smile spreads across my face. A smile not of happy amusement, but one filled with a grim sense of humor. Straight from the libretto of the gallows. Macabre and fatalistic. Just like the comicality I adopted while in the desert.

A 'Jack in a Box.'

"You're kidding?"

She smiles back. "No, I'm not. I kept some for the scattering up in White Ranch tomorrow, but you two belong together."

"I don't know what to say."

"You don't need to say anything. I want at least some part of him with you."

"Thanks. I think?"

"I know. It's weird, isn't it?"

"This whole thing is weird, Avery."

She rummages back through the tote and pulls out a large, rectangular metal sign. Reaching over to the desk next to the television, I quickly put the Tupperware container on it and take the sign from her. This offering—as if you could call these items gifts considering our situation—is almost as odd as the first. But it brings a much warmer grin to my face as I look at it for a long moment—

JACK ST

then back at her.

"Now that's funny, Avery. You know, we used to steal these things when we were kids. Stop signs, one-way signs, school bus stop ahead signs – whatever." I let my fingers travel over the letters, fond sentimentality washing through me.

"I remember them hanging in his bedroom like trophies," she says. "I don't know where he got this one; or whatever was going through his head when he grabbed it."

"Where'd you get it?"

"I found it in his storage unit."

"What a trip. Leave it to him to keep stealing them, even after we grew up."

"That was him."

"It was."

"And finally, I have—"

She bends forward and pulls out the last two items. Abruptly, my stomach lurches as I'm struck with an odd realization of how little stuff I have from Jack—a few pictures in a box in my basement, a stolen road sign, a Tupperware of ashes. And this.

"a picture of the both of you."

She hands it to me, and I look at it, warm love washing over me.

"Oh man. This was taken a very long time ago."

"Yes. You both look so young in it."

"Thanks," I say with a sardonic wink.

I gaze at it a few moments longer, the memory of us at the wedding together rushing through me. My wedding. A mock photo staged by the photographer of me pulling up one thread of the barbed wire fence around Rita's father's horse pasture. A gag of me trying to escape with Jack holding me back. Only both of us are laughing so hard, it's difficult to take the image seriously.

So long ago.

How can a lifelong friendship—all those decades—have so few scraps of tactile evidence?

I know why, of course.

"This last one," she says while gently laying a tattered, black and white speckled essay book on the bedside table, "I'd like to keep. But I brought it because I thought you might want to take a few pictures of it. That way at least you would have it in some form."

"What is it?"

"His journal."

I gulp, a shudder coursing through me. "Oh wow. Thank you, Avery. Yeah, I would. I would really, really love to read through them. I've been hoping to gain some more insight into what was going on in his head. Yeah, oh yeah, I would."

An uncomfortable pregnant pause clouds the space between us, and I rush to clear it. "Umm, can I get you some water or something? Do you need anything?"

She looks at me, and I see exhaustion in her eyes. Exhaustion interwoven with determination. The kind of determination that comes with someone knowing they must plow through what's facing them. Only then, on the other side, will it be time to relax, reflect, and begin the process of moving forward.

As we used to say in the Army, *"Mission first. Emotions later."*

"No. I'm okay. Besides, I ate too much at the memorial. I'm stuffed."

I turn sideways and stretch out on the bed lengthwise, shuffling and wiggling a bit to get comfortable while leaning on my right elbow. She follows my example and scoots to the headboard of the other bed, then turns sideways and stretches out. Propping her head up with two of the pillows, she looks at me; those steady eyes calmly, patiently waiting. It's hard to tell what's going through her mind and admittedly, I feel a little awkward. Does anyone know how to begin a conversation with their dead best friend's sister? I start where everyone else starts.

"Thanks for meeting me, Avery."

"No need. I wanted to. You were closest to him and even though you're not blood related, you're still family."

A well of sadness fills within me. Bubbling forth with a sense of embarrassment, and I don't know why. "Well, thanks anyway. I'm glad we're doing this. It's about time, right? I can't even remember the last time I saw you, but I do remember when you were born. Isn't that crazy?"

She grins. "It is. I only have few memories of you too, before my parents got divorced and I left with my mom."

"I remember that. That's when Jack and I were in high school. That was probably the last time I saw you."

She nods. "I think so. We didn't really come by the old house that much after that. My mom really took serious steps to create as much distance as she could from my father. And I think, sometimes, that was to the detriment of the boys."

She's so well spoken.

Like her mother and father.

Like her brother.

She shifts a little, getting more comfortable. It seems as if she's feeling more at ease now.

"Divorce is never easy," I say. "I know. I went through mine while I was in Iraq, and it wasn't pleasant. Took me a long time to process it."

"Jack told me about that. But you're okay now, right?"

I sigh. A wistful sigh. Thinking about those years always feels like weary resignation. "Yeah, I am. At first – for years – I was so angry, you know? Just filled with rage and depression. But you know what? Over time, I got to the point where I could forgive *both* of us for all the shit that went down."

"For a long time, I was angry too. Angry at both. My mom and I have a decent relationship now, but Jack and I took a long time to come together after the divorce, probably because of us living separately. And then of course, my father and Chris died."

"Those were rough years."

"Do you remember a lot?"

"Some. It was autumn of '88. I remember getting off the bus in the morning at school. And back then, you could go across the street and get some coffee at Store 24 before class. Big hangout place for all of us. We used to play hacky sack, smoke cigarettes, get high. Lots of fun."

She laughs and folds her hands over her belly. "You can't do that anymore."

"Really? That's a shame. But oh yeah, I remember. And word spread quickly. I think you know as well as I do those things, especially in such a small town, don't stay a secret for long. A buddy of mine, Jeff, pulled me aside and told me Jack was in the hospital, probably dying. Chris was already dead. He told me they found Chris' body about fifty feet in the woods and that he lived for about twenty minutes after the paramedics arrived. And the only reason they identified him was because of his fake ID." I squint my eyes and gaze at the ceiling. "Jesus, it's been so many years now. Jack and I were sixteen back then, so that means Chris was eighteen, right?"

"Yes," she replies.

"And how old were you then?"

"I was eleven."

We gaze over at each other, a few heavy moments laced with memories of shared, but separate tragedy.

A tangible connection for which neither one of us has words.

Blips

The hospital was antiseptic but with a faint odor of decay; the hallway deafening with its silence. Two nurses quietly shuffled from room to room, making the rounds while another sat behind a kiosk in a worn, fabric office chair, hunched over her paperwork.

I saw his breathing tube through the wire mesh glass of the door. An IV was taped to his arm. A pulse oximeter. A nasogastric tube. A heart monitor. Indecipherable numbers and wavy lines.

Blip…blip…blip.

His battered body, draped with sterile white blankets, was sunken into the railed bed. His arms and hands were motionless, matched only by his bruised, swollen, expressionless face. He was oblivious to the two vases of flowers and the several get-well cards on the bedside table. The sunshine which filtered through the half-drawn curtains.

I vaguely felt my watery eyes through the worry of sadness; I couldn't help my best friend. And a lump in my throat formed but I couldn't swallow. Knotted, tangled, I realized my breath had stopped because my anxious lungs were clamped, refusing to let go. Then, without warning, my anxiousness bloomed into downright, bottomless fear. My shoulders began to bunch. They were hot and tight with the sudden, agonized understanding that I didn't want him to go; that I didn't want him to let go of this world or vanish from my life.

But my invincible teenage mind couldn't plug in to what that meant. Only the dread of no more hanging out drinking beer, skipping school, carousing our town late at night with our BB guns, or egging houses on Halloween. No more listening to the Grateful Dead during a sleepover, exchanging Tintin books, watching *Night Court*, or building a teepee under a charred tree near our long dead forest fire.

This wasn't supposed to happen. Only old people pass away. They're supposed to. Like my grandparents when I was nine. My mom said it was just "their time"; that it was the natural order. Old first when they're wrinkled and hunched over. But not us. Not Jack and me. We're too young. We haven't even seen our twenties yet. Our thirties. Forties. Fifties. Time so far beyond my reach, it lived only in cryptic comprehension. An awareness of existence; nothing more.

Facing this shatters my defiance that we're somehow exempt from the fate of others. Those others who are different from us. The ones who are supposed to go. There was supposed to be time; time for us to be trucking partners, to get our first apartment together, to be able to buy beer without a college student, and to go to bars to pick up women. And everything, anything in between.

We were supposed to live forever.

Family

Avery shifts a little on the hotel room bed, settling in more comfortably, "What else did Jeff tell you?" she asks.

"That Jack had to be flown to the hospital. That they were doing over ninety when the car hit a telephone pole. That both of them were wasted."

"They cracked the car in half."

"I know. Split the frame. Anyway, a bunch of us, including Dee West, do you remember him?

She nods.

"We jumped into a buddy's car and went to the hospital."

"I haven't talked to Dee a while," she tells me, "but him and Jack kept in touch regularly throughout the years. My mom pulled me out of school, and we went down there together, where we met my father."

"I guess we missed you somehow." My fingers start toying with a wrinkle in one of the sheets. "You know, in some ways, looking back at it now, it was just plain stupid."

She frowns.

"What I mean is that essentially, Chris died for nothing."

"It *was* stupid," Avery agrees.

"And I remember visiting Jack when he got out of the hospital. I would go over to the old house after school and there he would be, sitting in his wheelchair just staring at the walls, his leg and arm in a cast, purple marks all over his body. I remember the seemingly endless months it took before he could walk. Even more months before he would smile or want to say more than a couple of words, more than just a vague nod of acknowledgment. Carl and him didn't talk much after that. And then, of course, he died."

"Did Jack talk to you at all? About any of this?"

Digging through the years, the road trips, the time spent living together, I find I can't recall any long conversations about this time. Everything feels hazy and I'm groping. "Not really. Not anything deep; substantial. I only remember him saying one time that he should've died instead of Chris." I smile helplessly., without humor. "It wasn't a topic that was brought up very much, Avery. I don't know why other than I think Jack didn't *want* to talk about it. I think he desperately wanted to leave it all behind."

"I think so too. Over the years, he only briefly mentioned what happened with our father; and he never talked about Chris."

We're silent for a few moments, our eyes wandering the pleasant, cream-painted walls.

"Jack found Carl, right?" I ask.

She nods. "Yeah. He found him lying in bed one morning. I think it was—"

"About six months after Chris died."

"Yes."

The fog lifts a bit, and I can recall it a little more clearly now. I see Jack that afternoon, and I'm listening to him telling me how empty it is to be alone in the house. I hear him telling me that he wants his mom to sell it. And that when we graduate in the spring, he's leaving New England for good. I keep on toying with the tangled bed sheet. "It always seemed to me that Chris was the golden child and could do no wrong."

"And a bully."

"You know he used to beat the crap out of Jack, right?"

"I never saw any of that."

"I did. It was tough to watch."

"Chris was extremely charismatic. Everyone seemed to love him no matter what he did or how he behaved. People seemed to be drawn to him."

"And that left Jack, the awkward one."

Silence between us. I have to stop twisting the bed sheet. "But you have a family now; all yours, which I think is great. How's that going for you?"

She runs her fingers through her hair, brushing it aside from her forehead, then shrugs. "I guess I would have to say, that like any marriage, we've had our ups and downs. But overall, we're happy. Calem's very down to earth and stable. Some might call that boring, but I don't. He's a good provider and a good father."

"He's a wonderful dude. I hardly ever meet someone so – Zen, you know? He just radiates it so naturally."

She laughs. "I know. The world could be exploding, and he would throw his arm around your shoulder, smile, and say, 'Well, isn't this just something to behold?'"

"And you have – what? Two kids now?"

She holds up her fingers. "Three."

"Wow." An image of me holding a baby in my arms flashes before my eyes. "I've never had any children."

"Did you want to?"

My eyes drift to the ceiling, then over the room. The 'Jack in a Box' flashes in the corner of my eye. "Not really."

"I think you may be missing out."

And now I know why I felt sad and slightly embarrassed when she said I was family. It's because I've always felt like I never had any sense of family. I'm not used to it. A foreign feeling because my parents and I struggled to be close. The bitter wounds of my mother's alcoholism and my parents' constant fighting always propelled me to move physically and emotionally further away. It dawns on me now that I always felt closest to Jack.

In many ways, *he* was my family.

"Maybe. But how are your kids?"

She nods to herself. "They're doing alright. Our oldest is graduating from high school this year."

"That's crazy."

A wistful smile. "It is. It was just yesterday she was eleven and killing our ears learning clarinet. Even longer since we were changing her Pampers. But I'm a little worried about her."

"Why?"

"It seems like she feels a little lost. You know – without direction."

I smile. "Well, I wouldn't worry if I were you. I think that's normal. Weren't we all when we were that age? I know I was. I know Jack was. But we found our way eventually. People always do. Jack seemed to."

A small grunt. "Yes and no."

My gut suddenly says it's time to dive right in. "What do you mean?"

"Well, you know he was getting divorced, right?"

"I did. We spoke about that on the phone – oh, I don't know, about two or three months before."

"And needless to say, it wasn't friendly."

"I got that from him." I pause and she waits. "You know, I've never even met her?"

"Saige?"

"Yeah. I don't even know her hair color."

A perplexed look washes over Avery's face. "Really? Why? I would've thought differently. That's very strange."

"Yes and no. Jack and I didn't talk for a while."

"Oh? Why?"

Books

Amazement was an understatement. Stupefied would've been more apt. Even dumbfounded as I watched him rummage through his storage unit on the outskirts of Denver. Boxes and boxes. Tools. Auto parts. Furniture. Posters. CDs piled neck high from the floor. And books. Books, books, and more books, all organized by his own method.

Whatever that was.

"What are you looking for?"

"A book I want you to read," he replied. Bent over, shuffling through books, his face was a concentrated study of an assiduous bibliosoph; an archivist foraging through the arcane.

"Sounds great, Jack," I said as I struggled to comprehend the amount of stuff, things, gear, goods, objects, and trappings in his storage unit.

"Don't mention it."

"Why are you always passing these books onto me?"

"Because you, of all people I know, understand the benefits of reading. Maybe better than I do. And I'm sure that you'll get some answers from this one."

He stood up straight and, as he handed me the book, he smiled and said, "Everyone should read this before they die."

His face beamed with both happiness and pride. Happiness

because he could give it to me, I'm sure. Perhaps pride because he was able to find it.

I took the book from his outstretched hand.

Coming Up for Air by George Orwell.

The everyday struggles of the common man.

Jack and I always stood together in at least this one belief. The belief that words could provoke important questions—Why are we here? What are we doing? Where are we going? How do I get there?—and walk us toward the answers. We appreciated the way books could suggest avenues for broadening our minds—our motivations, decision-making processes, doubts, fears, and sorrows—to help solve the mysteries of everyday reality.

The intricacy of what it means to be human and even the complexities of relationships.

"Thanks, Jack. I'm sure I'll love it. And I promise I won't toss it when I'm done."

His gift still resides on the bookshelf of my living room.

Next to my Tintin collection.

Revelations

The Drury Inn is almost silent as I think about what Avery asked me, *Why didn't we talk for a while?*

"He backed away big time," I finally reply.

"Backed away?"

"Yeah."

"Do you want to talk about it?"

"There's not much to say. It started before my own suicide wingding, but got worse after. We just grew more and more silent, more and more apart. It felt like he was drifting away and there was nothing I could do about it." I shake my head, the memory hurting it. "He, of course, explained it away as just being busy, time getting away from him, but it was more than that. We both knew it. He wouldn't talk to me and it really hurt. To be kept in silence is terrifying. So many possibilities went through me, but I couldn't get any…" I close my eyes and take a deep breath. "Anyway, he did explain why, what he was feeling – a few years later."

"I didn't know that. He never told me." She pauses. "What drove you to that point – I mean, was it any one particular thing?"

I feel as if the answer should be obvious and I look at her for a moment, wondering where she's going with this. Then I smile; a smile laced with both wistfulness and a sense of my past failings.

My own blunders and lapses. The smile of a person who's resigned to laughing about them now; now that they're behind me.

I look at her. "Shit, it really was a combination of everything – the war, the divorce, how everything just went so wrong. I felt like my life was a complete failure. Everything I had attempted to build just collapsed and was worth nothing. It's taken me years to get to where I am now – and I still don't even know where that is."

"That makes more sense to me now; you not being around much during the Saige years. You two had more in common than you both might have realized."

"That's true. But like I said, I've never even met her."

"So, I'm guessing you didn't go the wedding?"

Guilt ripples through me. And embarrassment and shame and remorse. "No. No, I didn't. He did send me an invite. As a guest. And I think that, in combination with the distance that had grown between us, it really hurt." My head sags as I wish time wasn't so linear. "I mean, he was best man at my wedding, and I was only a guest? And also, him and Rita were pretty close. He used to give her bear hugs whenever he would see her. So, no, I didn't go." I look up at her. "Was it a nice wedding?"

"It *was* nice. Simple. It was out in the open in a wonderful meadow up at White Ranch."

"Was that *his* decision?"

"Yeah. I think he conned her into it somehow. She wanted something more elaborate."

"I see. What do you know about her? Do you know her well?"

"Reasonably well. In general, she's a very private person. And she can be controlling. Dominant."

"She doesn't sound like someone Jack would hook up with."

"I agree. And you know what a social butterfly he could be. She's the opposite. She shies away from people and can be very awkward."

"So, what do think *was* going through his mind?"

Avery thinks for a minute, her brow furrowing, lips frowning. Concentrating. "He found himself in a very dark place he couldn't get out of. You seem to have managed to." She shrugs. "He didn't."

"A lot of people find themselves there."

"They do. And I know that he was desperately trying to find a way out of it, and all the anguish he was feeling. Shortly after he did it, I went through his apartment and found a whole bunch of self-help books."

"Well, he always did love to read."

"Reading, yes. But this was extreme. They were everywhere. A whole bookstore's worth; all of them with passages underlined and notes in the margins. I even found some in his storage unit."

"Jesus. So, what do you know about the divorce?"

She looks down at her hands. "What I know comes mostly from Saige. Jack never really talked about it. I don't know why. I'm his sister, but I think in some strange way he was trying to protect me."

"From what?"

"From reliving the past, from when we were children."

"I see."

She looks up at me, then sighs. "Saige called me multiple times throughout the last few years, mostly before she kicked him out and filed for divorce. She was really trying to work things through with him, but something was wrong – I mean, terribly wrong with him. And she would call me because she thought maybe I could get through to him or give her insight into what was ticking in his mind."

"Never easy with him."

"No. And I think for a long time—"

"They were together for how long?"

"About ten years. And they were happy, until the last five when things went downhill."

"The same as Rita and me."

"I guess. Anyway, it was within the latter half that their first child was born; the second came two years later. That's also when his drinking began to increase; slow at first, but still noticeable."

She pauses and looks at me.

I can't tell what she's thinking.

Then, I say, "Jack and I were always around booze in some form or another. I had my bout with it, that's for sure. After the war, I spent almost twenty years drinking heavily. It was only when I had to go to the hospital for high blood pressure that I had to give it up." I grin, a smirk brimming with self-mockery. "In the end, trauma, stress, and booze did me in."

She nods. "Well, there were several incidents that built on each other, and I think everything peaked shortly after their second was born. Saige couldn't take it anymore, especially after what happened."

"Such as?"

"They decided to remodel the kitchen and they had a lot of disagreement with how to go about it, which cabinets and appliances to buy, that kind of thing. Then, one night, he came home from a bar drunk off his gourd." She pauses. "Saige told me it was about two in the morning when she was startled awake by an ungodly banging. So, naturally she went downstairs to have a look. She said it was terrifying. The cabinets had been ripped from the wall and thrown all over the floor, the faucet was gone from the sink, the microwave on its side over by the table. And there was Jack, in the middle of everything, with a sledgehammer pounding away at what remained of the countertop. And of course, the baby woke up and was screaming. Can you imagine?"

Shocked, I take a deep breath and consciously relax the tension in my thighs. I wonder what must have been in his head to generate so much out of control destruction.

"No. I really can't. I can't picture him ever doing something like that. So, what happened then?" I ask her.

"They had a huge fight, and it was a mess. Eventually, he collapsed and passed out, but it scared the hell out of her."

"What else?"

"He calmed down for a while after that night, promising to be better. Then, a few weeks later, the same thing happened, only this time he was virtually uncontrollable. She told me he threw all the living room furniture out the window."

Looking at the tangled sheets for some sort of answer, I shake my head. "Jesus, Avery, what the fuck?"

"Yeah. He threw a chair through it; then the rest followed. They had another fight, and she threatened to leave."

"But she didn't?"

"No. When he sobered up, they talked it through and again, he promised to do better and to quit drinking. And he did. For a short while. But soon he was back at it."

Incredulous, a soft whistle escapes my lips. "So, what was the breaking point?" I ask.

"She had errands to run one afternoon, and he stayed home to look after the baby – the second one – and when she came home, she found him passed out on the couch, an empty bottle on the floor next to him while the baby was upstairs."

She looks at me and I don't know what to say. None of this sounds like the man I knew. Eventually, I murmur, "This is so fucked up."

"That's not all. After he shot himself, she discovered that he had multiple traffic violations pending."

"Like?"

"Speeding. Careless driving."

"How did she find out?"

"The cops told her while they were interviewing her afterward."

I'm now almost speechless.

"The worst was that they told her he barely escaped arrest one afternoon because apparently someone cut him off on the highway and they played road warrior for a short bit before they both pulled over. He got out of his car and threatened the guy, then punched him in the face. That's when the guy called the cops."

We look at each other for a very long time.

"I'm surprised she stayed with him for so long," she says. "I can't say that I know many people who would."

"Nor do I."

"But she finally filed for divorce when he lost his job with the state. I'm surprised he kept it so long after showing up drunk for about a month beforehand."

"So, after all that…"

"He got an apartment, and she basically did her best to shut him out of everything, even seeing the kids."

A door slams in the cavernous hotel hallway, startling me. It's soon followed by the muted chatter of a couple as they walk by us.

"I can't imagine what that must have felt like."

"I think, in some ways, it was a wake-up call for him. He tried all sorts of things to clean up; a few shrinks, which he hated, a couple of men's groups – all those self-help books. He went deeper and deeper into himself. Isolated more and more. I didn't hear from him for months until he reappeared about a month before he went up to White Ranch."

"Did you try to reach out to him?"

"Of course. I called, I don't know how many times. I went over to his place looking for him, but he always managed to blow me off somehow."

I'm not sure I want to hear anymore, but my need to know overshadows my fear of knowing.

"What was the last phone call like?"

"We had a real heart to heart. He told me that he was taking responsibility for his actions; that he was learning a lot about himself."

The soft hum of the A/C is now deafening. Fighting tears, I look down at the now knotted bed sheet bed sheet.

"The last thing he told me was – and I'll never forget this because I think it was the most important thing he ever said to me – he told me, 'Avery, I've come to figure out that I've been broken ever since Dad and Chris died.'"

Looking her in the eyes, I can only muster a, "Whoa."

Her eyes roll toward the ceiling for a moment. I'm surprised at how cool, calm, and collected she still is. How we both are. She thinks for a minute, then drops her gaze back to me. "Whoa is right. That's some seriously heavy shit. Do you think that's why he did it?"

I contemplate for a moment. "Well, I don't know. But I'm starting to see a cumulative effect going on here; from when we were kids and building over the years."

She nods. "I think the past never really leaves us. You don't just leave it behind; get over things. And I think Jack never made peace with that. I think he was stuck. I think that he really tried to somehow..." she pauses, obviously grasping for the right words, "...to somehow atone for all the family pain. But was never able to. And since we didn't have a decent family growing up..." she ends with a shrug.

"I would add his personal endeavors too."

"Right. When his own failed, personal and otherwise, everything crashed in on him. Everything was like one huge boulder of failure and pain. So he went down the rabbit hole and couldn't come up for air."

I chuckle. "That was a favorite book of his."

"What was?"

"*Coming Up for Air* by George Orwell."

"I didn't know that."

"It's a great book." I gaze at my fingers, my mind wandering back in time. "Do you know that it was the last book he ever gave me?"

"No," she says, obviously wondering at my wistfulness.

My eyes come back to her. "He gave it to me about a week before

I had my own suicide thing. He said it was a good one for me to read because it explored how harsh war can be and how the main character tried to recapture the past by returning home."

We look at each other, both of us sensing a certain irony.

"Do you think he was trying to tell you something?" she asks.

"Probably. Naturally, I didn't read it until after I went back to New England to reconnect with my parents and ground myself in some sanity." I smile. "But anyway…"

She smiles back. "But anyway, does any of this make sense?"

"I think it makes a lot of sense. Was there anything in his journals that shed some light on what was going on?"

"There was. Would you like to look at them, and take a few pictures?"

My mind is spinning; whirling with all that I must digest. "Yeah. Yeah, I really would."

Chess, Part Two

"Checkmate," he said with a frown. His grim tone was contradictory to what would be expected from another victory.

I stared at the board; at the emptiness of the squares where the fierce but futile battle had taken place. At my decimated army of pieces all huddled together as they mourned from the sidelines. I took a hit from the pot pipe and passed it to him. "Shit."

Jack smiled as the flame from the Bic hovered over the pipe, lit up his face. "My father taught me well."

"So, he did. Too well."

"Too bad he never got to see a geezer garden."

"Do you ever think about it?"

The mist of the pot we'd been smoking all night dissipated, and his eyes came into sharp focus. "About what?"

"Oh, come on, Jack. You know what I'm talking about."

His eyes pierced me for a moment, then, without looking down, he snatched up a slice of pizza from the box we had picked up from some place near the South Rim of the Grand Canyon. Through the cheese, he said, "Not really. What happened, happened."

"Yeah, but—"

"Like chess, my father thought about his moves ahead of time, then executed them with carefully thought-out logic. But in the end, it didn't matter much, because the world never balanced out for him. His reasoning never gave him the harmony he was looking for. All the logic and intelligence in the world couldn't help him because there was always something missing. Something he could never put his finger on."

"What was that?"

"The notion that intellect is nothing without imagination. Because of that, he was never able to bridge the gap between need and want. And, as a result, it feels like he was doomed to repeat not only history, but all the lunacy associated with what I would call a regulated delirium, aka, society. I seem to be following suit."

"I don't know about that, Jack. You seem to be doing alright bucking the system; at least as best you can."

"Maybe. I guess one way I've found to try and combat it, is to try and live fully without reservation, to take it all as insatiably as my stomach allows, and to constantly remind myself that even though I've largely thought my crises are the most important thing in the world when they're happening, they're not. Other people's, and the planet's, are doubtless more important."

I thought for a moment. "I think you have some really good ideas, Jack. You should be the writer, not me. You have a lot to share that's worthwhile."

"Maybe. But the sad fact is that, for all my thinking and talking, I've failed miserably at actualizing anything. I've spent too much time being lazy about staying in the present, or even the future, which is where I've needed to be. No balance. And in the end, my father couldn't live with that. So that's that."

"Don't be too hard on yourself."

He looked at me and didn't reply for what seemed like hours, then he breathed in deeply. "Okay, man. No need to keep listening to me blathering on like a bubble-headed boobie anymore."

I smiled at the memory of two nine-year-olds glued to *Lost in Space* reruns. The Robinson model family as they rocketed around in the Jupiter Two; *The Brady Bunch* in space with the reprehensible Dr. Smith as their unwanted stowaway. "Better than a deplorable dunderhead. Besides, your blathering is important to me, Jack."

He shrugged. "Well, at least he didn't have to do time in the spotted liver recreation center."

A vague twinge inside me suspected his nonchalance was a cover up, but I didn't want to pry too much. I didn't want to force him to talk more if he didn't want to. So I decided to call it a night.

"You gonna stay up for a while?" I asked.

"Yeah. I'm going to watch the fire."

"Cool."

As I picked my way over the darkened ground, across the ten foot distance to the tent, he spoke again. I turned and could see his head nodding, as if to himself.

"My father also never found harmony with his children, Dana," he stated flatly, still not turning to look at me. "He favored Chris over me. I know this. I always have. And I was telling you only a partial truth in New Mexico."

"New Mexico?"

"When we were talking about roadkill."

"I remember." I think for moment. "What partial truth?"

"I said that age, experience, and reflection has allowed me to be humbler as I've gotten older."

"Umm, okay. And?"

"It was only partial truth because I've also realized that I've been angry for a long time. Angry at my father and my brother. And, like so many before me, I took that anger out on a bunch of helpless frogs, on you, on myself, and throughout my life." He paused. "That was wrong. It was wrong because instead of making peace with it, I internalized, while inflicting my rage outward." He raised the pipe to his mouth, took a deep hit, then breathed out a billow of smoke.

"Don't be too hard on yourself, Jack. It's okay."

I waited, but he didn't say anything. Instead, he took another hit.

Not knowing what else to say, I crawled into the tent, kneeled on my water repellent, nylon bedroll, and watched him through the gap. Sitting on a rock, cross-legged, the pipe in hand, he stared over the campfire, under the kaleidoscope of Arizona stars. Eyes unfocused but fixed somewhere beyond the orange flames that danced equitable on his pensive face.

Inner Thoughts

Swinging my legs off the hotel room's bed and sitting up, I lift Jack's notebook from the bedside table. Resting it in my lap, I look at it, instantly feeling jittery. Jittery because a journal is meant to be a space in which to express yourself without fear of criticism or vilification or judgment. And as I open it, carefully beginning to thumb through the pages, I feel as if I'm violating Jack's sanctity. Without his permission, I'm snooping, exposing those private, innermost feelings most of us are, at the very least, reluctant to speak of. I can't help but feel somewhat treasonous.

I'm also afraid of what I might find.

But I remind myself that I'm not here to judge. To aim that self-righteous finger of condemnation. Because not only am I guilty of the same dark spaces, but I'm here to puzzle through what has been, what is, and I suppose, what could have been.

I take my time, turning one page after another. Avery sits watching, saying nothing. I'm surprised that the journal isn't filled from line to line. Margin to margin. But no. I'm finding random notes more than anything else. It reads more like footnotes from an outside observer, or a reference guide for a detached bystander. A disjointed register:

Set of reflections of self-loathing
funny lonely brave overwhelmed

entitled terrified undeserving arrogant

impatient paralyzed lazy

I continue to take all the blame.

Don't believe I deserve any happiness

A few pages are filled, but only here and there. Most entries have sporadic dates and times. Nothing of what I would call a narrative. Admittedly, I'm disappointed with the pieces. With what I anticipated would be a chronology, beginning with brightness, but descending into darkness is still nothing more than a puzzle I can't figure out. What I wanted was a step-by-step guide taking me on his journey. A story in which all the answers to my questions, and his choices, are finally revealed. Act one, act two, and act three with a coherent and cohesive ending, however bleak.

I'm still confused.

Snap.

I take a picture.

"This is interesting," I murmur, holding up the journal for Avery to see. "A chart."

She nods. "I think he was making a graph of all the ups and downs in his life. His way of creating a picture for him to examine and see how everything had transpired."

Snap.

Another picture and I chuckle. "That sounds like him. Always the analyst."

"Totally."

I point to a page. "And here."

Beat drinking!!!

Her eyes squint as she read. Then, she scooches up and crosses her legs, folding her hands in her lap. "He obviously knew it was a problem."

Snap.

Another picture.

"Yeah."

"But you know what's weird?"

"What's that?"

She thinks for a moment. "I'm trying to figure out how to put this."

"Take your time."

A long pause, then she speaks. "Jack knew his drinking was a problem. It got him fired, his marriage was ending – it basically destroyed everything. And I discovered from talking to other people that he was smoking a lot of pot; taking some mushrooms here and there, and that he was even taking Lithium."

"Lithium? That's used for things like bipolar."

"Yes. And mood disorders."

"Was that prescribed?"

"No, he got it from a friend. God only knows where the friend got it."

I scratch my chin. "Sounds sketchy, and awfully dangerous to me."

"It sounded that way to me too. But the strange thing is that when the medical examiner did the autopsy—"

"They did one?"

"For all suicide cases, yeah."

"And?"

"The toxicology report came back clean. Negative for all drugs and alcohol."

I stop flipping through pages, taking pictures, and look at her. "So, he was completely sober when he did it?"

"Completely. No traces of anything."

I turn a page. "You know, that almost makes it worse."

"How so?"

"Well, if he was all fucked up on something when he did it, then I could kinda blame the drugs; that he was out of his mind somehow; that maybe he really didn't mean to do it."

"He meant it. And he thought it through."

I nod. "Clean, sober intent."

"Yes."

I turn to another page and come across the very last entry. My heart stops for a moment, a lump gathering in my dry throat.

John Marshukin it is time for you to die. Your children couldn't care less. Your wife hates your guts. You've ruined everything that's good your whole, entire. worthless life. Wasted everything. You are a fucking piece of garbage shit.

DIE garbage Die

I read this entry over and over. And over. Time and time again while Avery silently waits. My mind can't comprehend his unforgiving, unyielding, maliciousness toward himself. A brutal self-loathing beyond what's fair and reasonable. A savage distortion that disregards the complex nuances of living. The difficult, yet rewarding, experience of being human. None of this pays homage to the man who soothed my sunburned knees or who was ravenous for life.

Why didn't he save any of that compassion for himself?

Snap.

I take the final picture and close the journal.

Avery stands, stretches, and picks up her purse. The now empty tote.

"You gotta go, huh?"

"Yes. I need to. It's late. It's been a long day. I'm tired and I should get home to the waiting fam."

"That's cool. I understand." A random thought jumps into my head. Perhaps not so random. "What happened to the gun?"

Frowning, she pulls the tote closer to her chest. "After the police were done investigating, they gave it back to me."

"That's fucking weird, Avery. So, what the hell are you supposed to do with it?"

"I know, right? Like I want the damn thing. Do you want it?"

"Why would I? I have no use for a gun anymore – especially that one. Those days are over. What are you gonna to do with it?"

"I don't know yet."

"Have the cops destroy it. It'll be one less gun in the world."

"That's a good idea. I'll do that."

We both walk toward the door. We're both out of words, haggard and mentally worn out from the day. As we ride the elevator to the lobby, I ignore the robotic courtesy voice.

Emerging through the front doors of the hotel and through the parking lot, we're soon next to her car. Parting after a long, tight hug, we hold hands while looking at each other. She looks down at the pavement, then up into my eyes. "He loved you very much, you know. You were brothers for life."

I nod, holding back my tears. My bottom lip trembles. "He loved you too."

She nods.

The warmth of her hands leaves mine and she turns to her car. The headlights blink once, then twice. She opens the door and looks back at me.

"I'm glad you two had each other."

She gets in, the door closing, the engine springing to life. I watch as she winds her way through the parking lot maze. Soon the taillights of her midnight blue Toyota Sienna vanish into the amalgam of the other cars.

I'm comforted that Avery and I have reconnected, have shared our feelings, our thoughts. Through her, I take solace in the knowledge that some part of Jack is still alive. Yet, a peculiar sense of the past with the present, that's left me intellectually and emotionally disheveled, lingers. Unsettling in a way that's difficult to put my finger on.

I give her a final wave even though I know she can't see me.

I'm going to miss her.

As I turn and walk through the waiting, open doors of the hotel, it hits home with me that, however reluctant, and at times indecisive I was, I knew deep in my heart that I had been looking forward to this trip. To be back on the road. To be with Jack.

I reach the elevators and push the up button, my eyes watery from exhaustion, hollow with emptiness.

But after hiking through, in those million moments of stasis, I know that everything is behind me. There are no more apartments together. No more gas station sandwiches or philosophy rants. No more high school antics or burning down acres of wilderness. Or gawking at buffaloes. Or white-water rafting. Or coyotes. No more adventures. No more insatiable zest for life. The whole shooting match and nothing less. Even the formal, designated time and space for reminiscence has ended. No more drinking cheap beers while joking about a funny thing Jack said or sharing warm smiles about touching moments.

We all return to our lives.

Absently strolling down the hallway, I open the door of my room and toss the key card on the nightstand with the awareness that I still feel old.

And I know that my time in Denver is over. The city's changed too much; I've changed too much. When I leave here tomorrow, like the war, I won't be coming back.

So where do I go from here?

To the one place where Jack and I always felt comfortable.

Nothing left to do but get on—

'You ready to go home?' Jack asks from the silken, plush armchair.

Feeling a slight tug at my heart, my conviction, I sit down next to him and look at the darkened ridgeline. *'I guess,'* I reply.

He muses for a moment, then closes his eyes. *'Perhaps Dana, death isn't so much about a ceremony for the deceased or a celebration of a life – or even clinging to the person through the past. Perhaps, as Orwell wrote, it's more about when you can't take in a new idea.'*

Listening to the Silence

The air was still somewhere outside of Moab as we sat on a ledge overlooking a valley and the drop below. Our bellies full of pizza, Jack's gaze was somewhere out beyond the majesty before us. Somewhere beyond the deep, gold sunset painted with streaks of burgundy and purple. He tossed a small pebble over the side of the ledge, and we listened to the tumble until it was lost in the silence. High above, an eagle screeched.

I turned to him. "We're gonna be back home tomorrow, aren't we?"

He nodded. "Yep. Back to the ants and the city life."

I looked back out over the seemingly endless painting of beauty. "I wish we could stay here."

"Me too. Life isn't as overwhelming here in this vast stretch of nothing. Here you can hope to find your identity and be yourself. Where you can try to overcome feeling like an automaton. Where you can try to realize you're not dispensable." He dropped another pebble, then continued. "And I've heard it said that sitting with the silence of oneself allows the spirit to climb out of the hamster wheel for a while; to inwardly perceive oneself with more clarity." A pause. "I'm almost at peace when I find myself in places like this."

A few stars began to appear above us.

"It has a lot to say – if we listen, that is," I told him.

He looked down and rested his hand on the rock next to him, a small unassuming, rust-colored fragment of rubble. "I guess that's true. And maybe then, there would be no fever for intangible purpose. No hurry. No inebriety with daily thoughtless hurrying or unmindful happiness. Maybe I could appreciate and imagine the simple percolation of time itself; the real rapture of life. Maybe there wouldn't be any need for feeling restless, even stupid inside."

I noticed the moon had risen—a fingernail moon.

He squinted his eyes as the sun slid beneath the burgundy horizon with one final splendid, yellow/orange flare. Silent for a few minutes, then, a relaxed tone, "Bottom line, I love it out here. There's no one to tell you who you should be or shouldn't be. No one to berate you. No one to tell you're not good enough, not smart enough. Not even anyone to elevate you. You can just stop time and come up with new ideas about how you want to live."

I felt as I did when we were driving through Kansas. Helplessly inept within my own inadequacies to help with the pain I saw in him; heard from him.

Where did it come from?

Maybe I should've asked.

Or maybe he wanted me to ask but was hesitant to tell me to do so. I don't know. And I didn't know what to say, so I asked him, "Do you want me to leave you alone for a while?"

"Nah, Dana. I'm glad you're here. There's no one else I can think of that I'd rather watch this with."

I thought for a moment, then asked, "Can you imagine living here?"

He sighed. "Probably not."

Interlude, Part Three – The Gentle Lapping of Despair

Quiet, as the Colorado evening deepened to night; a thickened darkness.

As I listened to the *whop, whop, whop* of the rotor blades.

And felt the desert air press through me; the dust swirl around me.

Why had I believed in imagination? In dreams? In adventure? Of a new life out west? In the solidity of marriage? In the faith I put in those around me?

I hadn't intended to end up this way when I joined. To find myself in the empty wasteland of my morals, judgment, and beliefs. To be washed up on the beach, dazed and dreamlike, after another post-traumatic wave. To feel so out of body because of depression, anxiety, hyper vigilance, rage, suicidal ideation, recurring nightmares, and survivor guilt. To use drugs and alcohol as a means to soothe my soul. To wipe out the flashbacks.

I hadn't intended to lose my humanity.

"Life's a bitch, ain't it kiddo?" said my father with a smirk, as he directed me to rake the leaves when I was ten years old.

The clock was late, and I was drunk. I needed to end this once and for all. That pervading force of post-traumatic stress that pushed me into a black corner of no escape.

Tick-tock. Tick-tock.

Push, push, push yourself beyond what you've known. Push, push, push yourself into a sweet, new land of peace. Push, push, push into nowhere.

A release into freedom.

A hymn for deliverance.

○

I paced the carpet of my bare apartment. The brief euphoria I felt after a couple of pulls from my pipe settled into a whirly, drunken high with my mind alight. Blurriness of alcohol tamed by the clarity of being stoned.

A fog had broken.

A clear place.

But through that sense of Zen came a more forceful inner voice. A voice that demanded even more of my attention. My hands and feet tingled. I had energy, although I didn't know where it came from. I should've been tired, but I wasn't. I was fueled it seemed by the activity in my brain.

For almost five years now, I had tried every day to put my best foot forward. To come to terms with my experience in Iraq. To blend back in and be awarded membership from the population at large.

I tried to keep my mind together—a sheer force of will to feel unchanged. A stubborn attempt to shove the pain and trauma into the background. But the desert was my breath, my blood; the pulse of my heart which gripped my tendons, my muscles, and oozed from my skin.

It was me. I was it.

Shouting. Explosions.

The psalm of war never ends.

As I took another sip of my Martini, I looked across the flight line of Camp Anaconda. Back and forth. Back and forth. Back and forth across the wide, flat expanse of concrete. After another glass of vodka, I turned and went into my shop, then through it, passing over the threshold of the back door where the makeshift smoking section was. The camouflage netting.

Hot and tired.

As I stopped in my tracks, my apartment came back in a flash.

○

My mind drifted in an ether, phased in and out of the present and the past as I sat back down on the couch—the free one I had inherited from the guy in the next apartment. Not being here was the spookiest part. Alone was the only space where I felt somewhat comfortable.

But the bogeyman was always on my shoulder.

And ghosts lived with me, *were* me.

They emerged along the beaten trails that line the irrigation canals, among the low-lying scrub brush or clearings, shrouded heads lazily swaying. A young son clung to the edge of a teetering, rickety seat.

Vanished into the foliage.

Whop, whop, whop went the rotor blades.

Vibrated hearts with teeth.

A spun death over the palm trees of Iraq.

And Block 15, Cell C-69s door stood open. My hooch. Me, hot, weary, and drenched, as I sat alone in a lake of gravel. A machine gun belt emptied somewhere out beyond the perimeter.

Whop, whop, whop.

The man, the woman, and their children.

○

One bullet, two bullets.

Three bullets, four bullets.

Five bullets, six.

Snap.

The cylinder clicked into place.

With an abruptness I didn't expect, anger and sorrow and confusion and guilt gave way. The waves no longer crashed upon the beach. Turmoil receded into the horizon. There was only the gentle lapping of despair and with it, peaceful emptiness.

Calm washed ashore as I stared at the loaded pistol.

On my coffee table, ready to go.

A Ruger GP-100 revolver with a four-inch barrel.

The hammer, the trigger, the cylinder, the polished rifling, the lead in the bullet casings would provide the delivery I needed.

○

My lips hugged the barrel. Sweet embrace. My teeth clamped down over the front sight, the muzzle rested on my tongue. The steel tasted sharp and bitter, like iron from a bleeding cut. A faint oily glaze blended with my saliva.

Thumb on the trigger, hammer cocked.

It was then I saw my father's outstretched hand. His expressionless face. I saw the smudgy, white futon mattress in the corner, flat and compressed from years of use. The mattress I slept on when I came home from the war. When I was homeless. When I was staying in my friend's garage.

I saw my rifle stowed in the arms room of Helena's National Guard airbase. That long rack of murderous carbon copies. I saw my parents at my college graduation. I saw Rita as we were getting married.

Jack was my best man.

I heard the melody of crickets.

Listen.

"But it's your life, I guess. I hope to God you can live with the consequences," said my mother after I told her I enlisted with the Army.

Tears in her eyes.

Bwoom. Brrrrrttttttt. Crack. Crack.

Bwoom. Fssssshhhhhh.

Chirp, chirp...chirp, chirp...chirp, chirp.

"Are you sure you want to do this?" Rita, my ex-wife, asked.

"It's time, Dana. I have to go," said Jack.

My father walked away in silence to smoke his pipe.

I had my poop in a group.

Hooah!

My body tensed; every muscle clenched.

There was only the thud of my heart.

Tears squeezed from my tight-shut eyes.

"I'm sorry."

Seeds

As if the Earth stood still, crisp eastern rays are beginning to bathe the mountains with the same gold of the previous evening. Aspens and pines, their vigorous green leaves and needles welcome the morning with a luminescent sheen. They shiver with gladness from a slight breeze; a breeze with a hint of what's to come.

Autumn is coming. I can feel it. Another cycle. A small, understanding smile touches my lips as I watch a bird, perhaps a hawk or falcon, no more than a speck, circling above. It seems to be overseeing the waiting landscape as it comes back alive.

A view only the west can provide.

I'm standing before the floor-to-ceiling windows of the Drury Inn after a hot shower and packing my gear. High above Colorado, the quiet feels solemn, insulated, as if I'm perched on a pulpit, removed from my species and its busyness below.

I'm alternating my gaze between the spectacular display of nature before me, and the niggling, antlike zip of morning traffic which winds its way through the concrete forest below. Cars of all colors swim on the thin rivers of grey asphalt. Semis glide down the E-470 Expressway. Delivery trucks rest under the branches of stoplights. Contrived trunks of bland skyscrapers cast long shadows, their glass windows hiding the small faces sipping coffee at desks, answering phones in cubicles, or grimacing at a jammed photocopy.

In the parking lot below, a young couple is talking. An old man is waiting for a dog to finish its business under a freshly planted, manicured sapling. And a bakery truck is parked near the automatic, sliding doors of the front entrance. Muffins, bagels, and cinnamon buns are being hand trucked down the ramp.

The bustle of Denver versus the unmovable, silent peaks.

I shift my weight to my other leg.

I'm suddenly reminded of when Jack and I used to play Boot Hill when we were kids. The wild west role-playing adventure game that first hit the shelves—and dared every boy to become a six-gun hero—in 1975. The version we played was published in '79. The third in TSR's line of fantasy, it never gained the popularity of Dungeons & Dragons, but for Jack and me, it was a treasure that no wizard or sword or scaly beast could ever hope to conjure up.

We pooled our allowance money. We bought the game—all the adventure modules, dice, and maps. Even small, metal figures. We created stacks of paper characters. Some good and honest, others downright dirty and mean. We stayed up all night and whispered to each other in the flashlight dimness of our bedrooms as we played out the dramas of our alter egos.

Scoundrels, bandits, gunslingers. Lawmen with silver badges. And scallywags of every type, their eyes red with greed, populated our imagined landscape. The clomp of hooves. The shrill canticle of spurs. The thud of boots on wooden planks. Dusty, wide-brimmed hats. Grizzled faces with prickly whiskers. Corks from amber whiskey bottles pulled out with teeth. Acrid, stale smoke from cigars. Ladies of the night, stuffed into frilly dresses and bodices in pool halls. Upright pianos bellowed out "The Old Gray Mare Ain't What She Used to Be" or "Bye Bye Blackbird" or "Lonesome and Sorry."

Best case, if you were a flannel mouth and didn't get yer hair in the butter, you'd stay above the snakes while havin' a hog-killin' time.

Worst case, it was always better to pull your shootin' iron than end up in the ol' bone orchard.

Around every corner of every saloon, livery, corral, mercantile, boarding house, or Chinese laundry danger lurked. There were bank robberies. Hangings and jail breaks. Wagon train ambushes. Banditos crouched behind boulders. Injuns in the hills. Rustlers over yonder. Cattle feuds. Rattlesnakes and cloud bursts. And treasure seekers searching for a hidden cache.

Lookin' to strike it rich.

"There's gold in them there hills," the old prospectors used to say. Their truth from the hearts of back-breaking, scant nugget fever. Their quarry for riches and independence. And I can almost imagine a wrinkly old, bearded panner with sun-squinted eyes and torn burlap pants spurring his mule down the slopes into town. A treasure map to a great fortune hidden in his pocket.

Almost.

Because this land is also unearthly gold in the form of a dream. A dream couched in the heart of a fable born from hope. A hope that coalesces from something nebulous into a firm belief, then supposedly willed into reality.

A pocket full of mental pictures.

A self-made direction.

A belief that these prairies and mountains can somehow thrust from their earth the answers to lingering, restless questions which live, ever elusive yet pestering, in the corners of longing. Questions of dissatisfaction. Of disquiet and unhappiness. A conviction that the answers will somehow lick the festering wounds of the past. Will settle any torment by putting dusty boots down on fresh, tilled soil. And to dynamite "what was" to mine "what can be."

Heart, body, and soul freed from weight.

I'm sure Jack felt the optimistic power of this dream when we first rolled the percentile dice for our wild west heroes. When we imagined we were outlaws and fast drew on conformance. When we took aim at convention. When, as a young man, he first decided to pack up his wagon and go west. To blaze a new trail within this tapestry of allegory for the subconscious. And I'm also now sure he felt a piercing, agonizing realization that the dream wasn't going to pan out.

When he found nothing branded on these brooding slopes.

Boxes, Part Two

In keeping with Jack's Road trip tradition of never traveling the same way twice, I'm heading northeast on I-76 toward I-80.

Watching the sun rise. Ever higher.

I'm driving through the stretch of plains between Denver and the border of Nebraska. The white lines sweeping by, as they always do, as I'm breathing in amber and benevolent morning air from the open window. As I'm leaving Avery, Libby, the Drury Inn, Denver, and the meadows of White Ranch behind.

The dreamscape loot of the mountains.

I have a long day ahead, and my mind is beginning to turn over the events of the last few days. So, I'm rummaging through a mental meadow of boxes. Like mining the basement before I left the east, I haven't been through these boxes in years. But unlike those celluloid moments, these ones aren't frozen in time. Rather, they're fluid; ever changing with the acuity that blossoms with age.

When I was young, and witnessing them, there was no way to look back with eyes that bore a broader, more adult discernment. I couldn't conceptualize any long-term damage which might have been done, let alone the motivations or reasoning behind them, only able to wince with pain and empathy at what I was witnessing. But now, I'm beginning to see with a little more clarity—from a new, broader perspective.

Sifting through them, I come across what I've been looking for—our childhood.

I frown as I sink further into my seat.

The top memory I have—perhaps because Avery and I just talked it over in the hotel room of the Drury Inn—is the divorce of Jack's parents.

O

High school. We're lounging across from each other in the living room of his house. He's on the couch. I'm in a plush, velour easy chair. The bong is bubbling while he holds the rim to his lips, as a Bic lighter is kindling the fresh bud of weed. Two glasses of chocolate milk rest on the coffee table between us. *History of the Grateful Dead (Bear's Choice)* is quietly strumming in the background.

Other than that, the house is silent; empty, but for the two of us.

"My mom is taking my sister. I'm staying with Dad," he states through an exhaled cloud of smoke. He leans forward to pass the bong to me.

I take it and light up while looking at him.

A deep inhale.

He's slumped on the couch now, folding his hands behind his head; eyes somewhere beyond the popcorn ceiling.

My stomach is turning. My thighs are tight. And I'm sad. Obviously, I don't have as many memories here as he does, but I've been so close to this family for all my seventeen-year life that I feel the weight of the change that's taken place.

The loss. The dismantling of everything built.

And I feel sad because I love my friend.

○

We're seven or eight.

I see his father sitting at his grand piano in the corner of the living room as we were playing with Jack's Mego *Star Trek* action figure dolls. He's Captain Kirk and I'm Mr. Spock. We're on a landing party mission to an exotic world, the alien Persian rug we're lying on a few feet away from Carl. The rug is the fabric of a dangerous alien maze, a test of resilience in which we're trapped, while his music provides the action soundtrack.

We've been hoping for a long time that someone, anyone, will beam us up.

The sun is filtering through half-drawn, cream-colored curtains. Carl's eyes are closed and he's softly rocking back and forth on the bench. He stops playing and picks up the bottle from the coaster perched on the edge of the piano.

His father drank a lot.

Rolling Rock beer.

○

Around the same age, in the living room, Carl is leaning forward on the couch. Jack, who's sitting cross-legged on the floor opposite him, moves his queen across the checkered board.

Carl sits up, his bristly, gravelly voice booming. "God help me, that's wrong! Chris picked this up in no time. Why can't you?" He moves his knight in response.

Hesitating fingers hover above the board. Finally, Jack edges a pawn forward.

"No, no, no. Be practical and don't waste time with silly moves. That won't get you anywhere in this game, or in life." Another move.

"I'm trying, Dad," Jack says, moving his rook.

"You're not thinking ahead. Put yourself in my shoes. What would I do? Use your head for something other than a neck decoration. Checkmate."

Jack's head droops. "I'm sorry."

○

I'm standing in the hallway of Jack's house, awkwardly shoving my hands in the front pockets of my chocolate brown corduroys, my eyes shifting from the floor to Jack, who's squinching from underneath a mass of wet hair. The bowl cut his mother's given him for as long as my twelve-year-old mind can remember. She's towering over him, toweling him off from a shower, intent on her task. Her task of drying his freshly washed body. Hands scrubbing the towel into his scalp. Vigorous. Snapping and lively.

She glances up at me. "He'll be ready in a few minutes, Dana. He still can't wash himself very well."

Jack, the awkward one.

○

We're on the thin, coarse sandy beach of our town's small swimming pond, the hot, summer sun blazing down on the placid water.

"I want to go out to where the big kids are," pleads Jack as he kneels in front of my mother who's sitting on a rainbow striped towel reading one of her horror novels.

His six-year-old face is crunched up in a scowl, his fists planted in the sand as his earnest eyes are taking in the view of the square, floating raft bobbing gently in the center of the pond.

Folding her book with a thumb as a place marker, my mother looks at him and smiles. "Then, why don't you?"

"My Dad says I'm not a good swimmer," he replies.

My mother reaches out and grasps his arm. "Nonsense. You can do it if you want to." Then, she turns to me. "Dana, why don't you teach Jack to swim out to the raft?"

I scoop another plastic shovel full of sand onto the mound in front of me. "But mom, I haven't finished my sandcastle yet."

"You can do that later. Be a good friend to Jack. He really wants to go. And you've been plenty of times."

I gaze at her for a long moment, the vision of my fortress on the beach, a deep moat as defense against the waiting regiment of green, plastic army soldiers clouding my vision. Then, with reluctance and a pouty voice, I say, "Okay, *okay.*"

"Are you sure?" Jack asks, seemingly to both of us.

"Of course," answers my mother. "I put Dana in a pool when he was a baby and taught him how to swim. He's a good swimmer. Besides, I'll be right here watching to make sure nothing bad happens." She pauses and pats his arm. "You'll be alright. I promise."

Burrowing my shovel in the sand, I get to my feet. "Come on, Jack. Let's go."

Together, we walk to the shoreline and into the water.

He doggy paddles. Face squinched up through the spray from his hands. But determined, he makes it.

One arm around each other's shoulders as the beaming pride of his blue/gray eyes shines, reflecting brightly from the shiny aluminum of the raft. Side by side, our feet dangling in the water, we watch the other kids splash about.

○

Bozeman. In our early twenties. I've moved up from Denver and am going to school at Montana State. After considering Jack's advice, I'm majoring in Literature and Writing. A response to his warm, earnest encouragement to be an author and write something worthwhile.

And he's visiting for a few days.

It's around two thirty in the morning and the bars have closed. So we're walking back to my apartment along the sidewalks of downtown, and under the sporadic fluorescent streetlamps. Like this memory, I'm foggy. Unlike this memory, I'm foggy from a night of drinking and playing pool. Jack beat me at multiple rounds of eight-ball.

Out of the darkness, a college student emerges. He brushes past us, in the process bumping my shoulder, and mutters, "Look out, dickhead."

Lightning fast, Jack swings around and jabs a finger at him. "What's your fucking problem, man?"

The student doesn't bother to reply.

Jack starts after him. "Hey, I'm talking to you, asshole. I'll kick your ass into the pavement, motherfucker."

Behind him now, my arms are encircling his waist, my heels digging into the sidewalk in an effort to restrain him. Jack' s unbelievably strong; he's been training for the Forest Service.

"C'mon Jack. Forget it. Let's go. Who gives a shit what he says?"

I feel his body relax and, after a minute, goes limp altogether. I loosen my grip on him. Then, we turn and resume our trek home.

"You're not a dickhead," he says.

O

After school, when Jack and I are eleven years old, we're playing the game of Life in the basement of his house. Without warning, Chris bombs down the creaky, wooden stairs and goes straight to Jack. He grabs Jack by the upper arm, yanks him away from our game, and slaps him around the head. Then, he laughs and disappears up the stairs as fast as he comes.

"At least he only slapped me this time," Jack smiles while he spins the wheel.

○

I'm watching Chris throw my stolen winter jacket into the branches of a tree. High. Way beyond my reach. My mistake. The school bus was warm and stuffy, and I had taken it off. I couldn't get it back, his older arms easily fending me off while insulting me to tears, beginning with bubble gum in my hair and continuing with, "Fuckin' loser."

○

I'm watching Jack giving away the kittens to a kid and his parents. Born one night during a keg party, he's been nurturing them for months. Raising them. Naming them. Adoring them. And now, Carl is insisting that he give them away.

"But—" Jack pleads.

"The cats have to go."

○

We're seventeen, and it's our first semester of senior year in high school. Within the last year, Chris and Carl have died. Joan and Avery have moved out and are living separately, leaving Jack alone in the former family home. October or maybe November, and Jack's kegger is getting late into the night.

It's late in the evening and Jack's been wrestled away from me by a couple of other drunk kids. Struggling, but eventually, grudgingly, resigning himself to be escorted to the lawn outside, the revolver he had been aiming at me taken from him. I'm trembling so much

I have to put down the red plastic cup I've been clenching, spilling beer on the end table in the process.

This one I've always struggled to remember. Most of the time, it feels as if it's a dream more than anything else. A foggy place I seldom go back to.

After all these years, I can't remember what we argued about.

○

Three months later, after graduation from high school, we're hugging.

The former family home is sold, and Jack's moving to Colorado.

"It's time, Dana. I have to go."

○

The mountains are dimming now; almost out of sight. And the Nebraska state line is approaching.

What do I make of all this now? What am I feeling? Sadness? Anger? I only know that something is beginning to stir in my gut.

So I wander through this mental meadow.

Over and over.

Over…and over again.

Three Big Fears

"What's your big secret?"

I hesitated, not wanting to tell him. It might be a betrayal to the image he had of me, and I didn't want to ruin that. But I took a deep breath, then let it out with a sigh. I might as well. He was, after all, my best friend and I trusted him. "I'm…"

He waited patiently.

I finally let it out. "I'm afraid I'll never have approval from my father."

Obviously curious and interested, he cocked his head. "How so?"

I looked out at the sharp, rugged ridgelines; the stars of the show along the Sawtooth Scenic Byway. And marveled at how they both carved through the Boulder Mountains. Sunrise, midday, sunset, or even in the middle of the night, there was never any breath left after even the smallest gaze. An elk in a small field swiveled its head as we drove by.

Dispassionate. Unruffled. Brown eyes met blue eyes for a split second.

I turned back to Jack. "Well, you know how he fought in Korea?"

"I do. But how does that fit in?"

My brow was furrowed with embarrassment, a lingering unwillingness to even admit my feelings to myself. "He was always so hard on me, so – removed from me, like I could never reach him. And my parents never really liked each other."

"I remember."

"So, I've always wanted to do something that would bring us closer; that would connect me with him somehow."

"And how would you do that?"

I laughed. "Well, I've thought about joining the Army."

He laughed in return. "Now, that I'd like to see. Talk about a round peg being stuffed into a square hole."

Playful indignation shot through me. "Oh, come on, Jack. I could do it."

"I'm sure you could *do* it. Of that I have no doubt. I just don't think you'd *like* it. You'd end up like a Hawkeye Pierce."

"Maybe."

He mused for a moment. "I wanted to join the Marines."

"I remember."

"They wouldn't take me because of all the steel in my body."

"I remember that too."

Silence fell between us. Then, I turned to him. "Maybe I will. I've been dreaming of it ever since we were kids. Imagined it, fantasized about it, built it up in my mind of what it would be like to wear a uniform. To be someone important my father would be proud of. But I have to admit, it's kinda scary."

I looked out the window.

We rounded another bend of the road, and he smiled. "I think you have what shrinks call performance anxiety. It's the same thing that people fear when they have to get on stage to give a speech or something." A quick glance. "Don't worry. If it's any consolation, you're not alone. They say there are three big fears that defeat people – criticism, loss of love, and of course, death."

"Sounds like we're all just one big bunch of fears. What's yours?"

Passing in the Night

The sun has just set as this day of driving wears on. I take in the endless plains with its silhouetted dotted trees. The peeps of sparse, distant light from a house, a restaurant, gas station, or other lone outpost of humanity. I breathe in the darkening of Nebraska with its wide burgundy sky punctured by the stars.

Darkening, like my mood.

But the sky is a marvel. So open, but astonishing with its power to envelope, not only the body, but the mind within its infinite solitary guardianship; an endowment only the prairie can provide.

But Jack never liked the plains. He thought it was boring. But, unlike him, I've found being here soothing. That satisfying insignificantly significant feeling. Important within my own anonymity. A tourist of my meditations; provoked by silently passing through the darkness while everyone else sleeps. A certain dreamlike thrill.

In the past, when I've traveled at night, I've felt a heart-pounding reanimation. But, in this moment, I find it gloomy.

I glance at Jack. *'Let's talk.'*

'Shoot. I'm right here with you,' he says from the empty passenger seat.

'That's not funny, Jack.'

He shrugs and grins. *'You're right. Admittedly, that was dark humor.'*

I turn to look at him, slightly irritated at what I perceive to be his whimsical attitude toward such a serious subject. I decide not to indulge him further. So I plow on.

'Before I start in on this, please know that, as much as what I'm about to say may seem cold hearted, I never want to hurt you, Jack – although I probably have throughout the years. But hear me out because I need to get this off my chest and into the open air.'

He settles back in his seat. *'Okay. I'm listening.'*

'So, Jack, here's the deal. As plain and simple as I can get it.' I pause and take a deep breath. My chest feels tight, my thighs tense with the energy in me. *'The bottom line is that – man, I'm just so motherfucking angry with you. I'm so goddamn angry because you ripped me off. You ripped us off. You stole the rest of our lives together.'*

'Well, Dana—'

'Enough,' I explode, slicing my right hand through the air. I feel the heat rising in my face. *'It's taken me a long time to work this through in my head and now it's your turn to listen. I don't want to hear any more philosophy right now. Not today. It's my fucking turn at the pulpit. Got it?'*

I pause again and gauge where he's at. He seems placid, understanding, and patient while he gazes at the passing night. *'I'm sorry, Dana. Go ahead,'* he says finally.

'Good. So, now that you're dead, Jack, I'll be the only one to remember. Those times when we picked raspberries with migrant workers in the mountains of Utah for gas money. Or watched the Northern Lights up in Montana. Or even that time we pranked a student driver by pretending to be asleep at the wheel.'

I'm behind a car now. Just two vehicles on an otherwise empty highway; separated but together.

'Or when we listened to that toll booth operator in Kansas tell us about his UFO encounter. Or even sledding down Horse Barn Hill.'

Yanking at the wheel, I step on the gas, jerkily switching lanes at the same time, passing the car.

Seventy-five miles per hour.

My voice is rising, my body flushed. I feel almost feverish.

'In other words, Jack, I'm left to remember alone. And I fuckin' hate that. Now, I can only tell our stories to other people. But it's not the same. It's just not fucking the same.'

My vision closes in on me.

Eighty miles per hour.

'And another thing. Who's gonna be my best friend now, Jack? I feel half dead. Like we used to say on the phone, no matter where we were, no matter what we were doing or feeling, we knew we were with each other; that we could feel the other across the miles? How many fuckin' times, Jack?'

He shrugs. *'A lot.'*

'Too many for me to count. How do ya like that shit? I don't. I can tell you that.'

The other car is behind me now, receding in the rearview mirror. It occurs to me that the person I just passed will always be a stranger to me. Every minute detail of what makes them all that they are.

I have to consciously take my foot off the accelerator.

Seventy-five miles per hour.

My vision clears.

Seventy miles per hour.

Back to cruising.

My voice lowers; subdued now. Almost ominous with my melancholy.

'And you know what? Ever since the night when Libby called...' my head quakes, my eyes beginning to fill with tears, *'...after forty-seven motherfucking years of knowing you – Jesus fuck. Who's gonna be my best friend now?* My lips are trembling. *'Oh God, what am I supposed to do?'*

I look to the passenger seat for answers. The empty passenger seat.

Empty but for the 'Jack in a Box.'

Shafer Road

"Hey, check that out," he exclaimed, as he thrust his finger past me.

I swiveled my head, my eyes looking to where he pointed. "What?"

"That road. That's Shafer Road."

"So?"

He looked at me with incredulity. "It's only one of the coolest roads ever constructed, Dana. It winds its way all through the canyons, with views of this planet we'll probably never see again." He paused. "We *have* to drive it."

I laughed. Jack, ever the tour guide.

"There's a sign over there that says it's four-wheel drive only," I said.

"So?"

I felt like I was being challenged, put on stage; a small lump of indignance parked in my gut. I stared at him for a moment as I wrestled with it. Then, I decided to go with the flow and ingratiate him. Anyway, part of me was curious. I didn't bother to answer his question as I shrugged. "Okay. Let's do it."

"Awesome."

He swung the wheel, and the Mustang pranced onto the gravel.

The Shafer Trail Road.

Full of extreme switchbacks winding up and down, through the brick red rocks, the towering crags with brush clinging to the edges of drop-offs, it's not a place for the faint hearted. Steep. Low overhanging rocks. Sharp boulders of every size protruding from what feels more like a trail.

Both spectacular and frightening.

With wide eyes, I tried to take in every sight, tried to implant them in my mind so as not to forget a single moment. We drove in silence for about a half hour, each of us subsisting on the scenery while we traveled up, then down.

Then up and over, back and up. Then down and over.

Screech.

The Mustang's underside scraped a rock as we were jostled in our seats.

I turned to him. "So, what's yours?"

"What's mine what?"

"What's your big secret? Your big fear?"

The road had begun to narrow, and around the bend of a switchback, he waved his arm out the open window. "This is where they filmed the ending to that movie, Thelma and Louis," he informed me. "It's about two thousand feet to the bottom."

The road narrowed more. Another switchback.

"Do you think we should turn around?"

"Nah. Not yet. Let's see what's up around the next bend."

And narrower.

Screech.

Another rock. Another jostle.

We drove in silence for a while, crept along at no more than ten miles per hour.

While I gazed at a jutting boulder that beetled over my side of the Mustang, I said, "I think one of the biggest fears that people have is letting go."

Another jostle.

He nodded, but his eyes never left the road in front of us. "Agreed. My feeling is that it has to do with need."

Thwomp.

The Mustang jolted through a pothole as the road narrowed even more. It was now almost a single lane.

"Whattya mean?"

"I've noticed that our need to cling to life leads to us not being able to let go."

Screech.

Another jerk.

"I can see that," I said. "That makes a lot of sense."

We were going up more steeply now. The tires of the Mustang slipped, gained traction, then slipped again. The back end slid a few feet to the right; Jack, in response, stepped on the gas. The tires spun, tried to find some foothold. A lurch forward.

Grup.

My chest tightened. "Are we good?" I breathed.

"Oh yeah. Just fine."

More steepness.

"I think one of the biggest is often overlooked," Jack went on as if oblivious to the Mustang's labor. "If we don't let go and accept the inevitable, we begin to slowly die from within. A vicious circle's created that's ultimately self-defeating."

As we crested a rise, I looked out over the vast horizon. Hundreds of feet below us, the thin silver river snaked through the flat canyon. The sun sparkled on the water. Clumps of tiny trees. Beyond, on the other side of the canyon, the landscape went on for as far as I could see. Colorful mesas. Irregular, whimsical buttes. He was right. This was incredible. I could see for at least one hundred miles. A mini–Grand Canyon.

"Oh, fuck," said Jack.

We had just rounded a bend and there sat a huge boulder. A roadblock; time to turn around.

Jack sighed and I could hear the disappointment in his voice. "Guess we gotta go back down."

"It's okay, at least we made it this far."

"True dat."

He swung the wheel, and slowly maneuvered back and forth, back and forth, until the Mustang was turned fully around. An arduous task given how thin the gravel road had become. Had the road been any thinner, we would have ended up going in reverse the whole way down.

"Anyway," he said, "fears, needs, and wants transcend how we deal with life and death. They play an integral part in how we deal with relationships as well, both platonic and romantic."

"Oh yeah?" I winced.

Thwomp.

Another pothole.

"Yeah. We often approach a relationship with need. We feel undeserving somehow and the hope is that the other person will fill that void." Smooth, as if on automatic, he stepped on the brakes and the Mustang slid. Its tail end swung out, then straightened. "And all relationships come with a burden of some kind or another, so I prefer being practical and using a cost benefit analysis to figure out if it's worth it for me to get involved."

I gripped the edge of the windowsill. "What the hell does that mean?"

"I look at all the traits a person has to offer, and what they need or want from me; what I might be willing to give or not give. Then I decide if they're worth my investment. In other words, whether the cost to me is worth the benefit of being involved."

He swung the wheel slightly left, then back again, avoiding a rock.

I frowned. Somehow this didn't sit very well with me. I couldn't grasp the idea of someone on a chart to study. "Dude, that sounds awfully cold and removed. I think I'm more of a romantic. Maybe the better way to go into something like that is to be comfortable within yourself first, then you have a desire to share yourself. Maybe this way, your wants will make you feel deserving enough."

"Maybe. But I'm only being pragmatic, Dana. Because, in the end, love will never be enough."

We rounded a bend, passed more rocks. Large ones.

"How close are we to the edge?" he inquired.

Now being on the canyon side, I poked my head through the open window. My heart stopped as my eyes looked straight down the canyon wall. "Umm, well..." I swallowed, my throat dry and chalky.

He looked at me. "What?"

"Our tires are almost halfway over the edge of the cliff."

"Uh, oh."

My heart began to thump in my neck as I watched a few small rocks and pebbles slide down the cliff. They disappeared, and in a flash, for no apparent reason, I wondered what it would be like to drive off this cliff at high speed.

The Mustang shifted, and I felt it tilt a bit.

My thighs tightened even more.

We crept along in silence, the sun becoming unbearably hot.

I peeked back over the side of the door and breathed a sigh of relief. Our tires were now only an inch or so over the edge. I felt dazed and in a trance, my mind still trying to understand why we hadn't slipped over the cliff.

Thwomp.

Another pothole; a small one on his side.

"What were you saying?" I mumbled.

Calmly, he answered, "I was saying that I've felt a desire for a deep relationship many times in my life, but doing my own cost benefit analysis, I'm not sure I'm over my needs."

An anemic smile crept onto my face. "I don't think you're alone in that."

"My problem is that I feel too paralyzed because I'm terrified of being seen as a failure."

"You get us out of this, and I'll never see you as a failure."

Silence.

I closed my eyes, my mind filled with images of us and the Mustang tumbling down to the bottom of the canyon. Then, without warning, from nowhere and everywhere, calmness washed over me. I felt blanketed with comfort.

The road widened, and I heard Jack take a deep breath. One of fulfillment; not fear. Then he looked at me. "Are we good?"

I peeked out the window. "Yep."

Two hours later, down at the bottom, by the edge of the main road, the Mustang idled with a purr of relief. We smoked cigarettes, both of us somewhere else.

And I was astonished at how calm he was; how calm I was.

In that moment, as my quaking, adrenaline fueled hands lit another cigarette, I loved him more deeply than I had ever realized before. I breathed in the smoke and sat back in the passenger seat. I knew then that no matter what, I had always felt safe with Jack. That no matter how we pushed the boundaries of anything we did, he would always be with me.

I would never be alone.

I watched as Jack tapped his finger on the top of the steering wheel, his face bunched up in a contemplative scowl. Above us, a hawk screeched over the idle of the Mustang's engine. The rest of the landscape, along with me, waited.

Then, he turned to me and said, "My biggest secret, Dana, is that, with all the shit with my family, all the crap I carry around, if I stop driving my life so hard, I'm pretty sure my past, and everything else, will slam me in the ass once and for all." He paused, then sighed. "But also, that I've known all along I'll never be able to outrun the sun. That it's a worthless, futile effort and yet I've been waxing and milking time to the point of nausea to do anything different. That because of this, I'm pointless and I'm never going to be anything more than an asshole who's running away."

He investigated me deeply. Then, his face softened, his eyes glimmered, and he reached out to grip my shoulder. "But Dana, these times I've had with you, what we've shared over the years, takes all the bitter out of the bittersweet."

He returned to gazing into the horizon and smiled. A smile that told me, without reservation, that we were connected beyond life and death.

"Let's go get a burrito," I suggested.

The gear lever slid to Drive. "You bet. I'm starved."

Forget Me Not

After catching a few winks at a rest stop close to the border, I'm now past Nebraska, and speeding through the Midwest into Iowa. The same country where, a few years ago while stopping for gas, I was scrutinized by every eyeball at the pump and in the store. Sized up with blank expressions of open, barely-masked disdain at my tie-dyed T-shirt and long hair which I'd tied back in a ponytail.

Despite my Veteran plate. So much for the melting pot.

I'm also back in the humidity, the recognizable influence of the Mississippi River pervading, only not quite as potent as down south.

I've just passed the birthplace of John Wayne—now a museum in Winterset. A few miles off the highway, it's a monument to an American hero who rose to become the centerpiece of pioneering and rugged individualism. An avant-garde icon of colonization; of industrious establishment squatting. A real, honest to God, tell-it-like-it-is man of all men.

Who also changed his name.

Maybe Marion was too feminine.

I zipped by the big, green exit sign without even a blink.

And here, on I-80, there is no gateway to the east. In America, you can only go in one direction; at least in your mind. West. Forward toward that better future. To backtrack and head east seems to be an unwritten blasphemy; an affront to getting ahead.

A fuck you to moving forward.

I grimace. East. West. Seriously? Does it matter to me anymore? Why am I rushing? Pushing so hard? I honestly don't know.

I used to savor these moments on the road. Taking in every drop like a cowboy or wagon trainer who had just found an oasis after wandering through a vast southwestern desert. Now, not so much. Now, underneath, there's a growing sense in me that, as much as I'm enjoying being here, the thrill of feeling my wheels spin is clouded with something else. A dichotomy I can't explain yet. Do I not feel the need to drive? To find something? Anything? Did I even know what I was looking for in the first place? I don't know.

Maybe I'm beginning to see more clearly why Jack and I traveled and lived the way we did. Because, despite my backward direction, a new horizon seems to be lurking; coming closer as I'm confronting the rising sun. It blankets my face with brilliant heat; warms me with a familiar, yet unfamiliar panoramic ideology which is beginning to edge over the rolling hills. Through the silver rivers. Under the hazy air, but above the oceans of corn.

But surprisingly, I'm not tired. My bladder is calm and quiet. No achy bones. And, despite my outburst last night, Jack's been back since this morning. In his usual place—the empty passenger seat.

'After last night, I wasn't sure you wanted me around,' he says.

I smile. *'I do, Jack. I need you.'*

Mostly silent up until now, with only random, mundane chit chat here and there.

More favorite billboards:

Save The Babies

'From whom?'

'I think that depends on your point of view,' mulls Jack.

Battles Are Won Within Join The Marines

'A paradox of conviction?'

'Ironic that they're next to each other,' states Jack.

Tired of the same old tunes—and needing some new music in my life—I reach for the stereo and turn off the Grateful Dead.

Jack's brow furrows. He seems deep in thought. He eventually turns to me, and says, *'Do you suppose there's a certain irony in the fact that I shot myself?'*

I smile grimly as a montage of images swiftly pass before me—loading my pistol, my balls hanging out of the hospital gown, Jack's suicide note found in his car, the peaceful calm of White Ranch. *'How so?'* I ask.

'Well, that night, when I came to pick you up at the hospital, I was so angry with you for being such a fucking moron wanting to kill yourself. Back then, I didn't understand why you'd want to; how you could find yourself in a place to even think it. For the first time, I felt as if I didn't know you. And I wanted to help you so badly, but I couldn't. Sure, I put you to bed and sat with you, but I was terrified. So I did what I've done so many times in my life – I ran from it.' He pauses, shaking his head. *'But the irony is that I went ahead and did the same damn thing.'*

'It kinda is ironic, isn't it?' I reply while reaching for a cigarette. Lighting it with my Bic, the smoke swirls out the half-open window. *'I think that's something we should talk about.'*

He nods.

I take a deep drag, then exhale, thinking carefully of what I want to say. *'First off, I'm going to assume that you reasoned everything, as you always did. Like with our chess games, you examined all the angles and their consequences, and then, using the cost benefit analysis, you made your move. Am I right so far?'*

'Yes.'

So I go on, *'And just like me, you felt backed into a corner. So, one day, who the fuck knows when, you decided there was no point in playing the game anymore; that exhaustion with outwitting your problems took over; that you were probably sick to death of being a fuckin' pawn and taking jabs all your life.'*

A gush of sooty exhaust rushes in the window as a semi passes us. *'You're right about that.'*

I take another drag and glance sharply at him. *'And also, like me, you probably felt you were left with nothing but the only logical decision you could make. You decided to do what your father did. What my father did. What I did.'*

'Still right.'

'Checkmate buddy, with whatever dignity you had left. And like me, you probably felt a sense of relief. I know I did. I know my thoughts became clearer once I decided. More peaceful.' I squint at him while taking another drag. *'You with me so far?'*

'I am.'

'Good, 'cause here's the fucking deal.' I jab my cigarette into the open ashtray and abruptly press on the brakes, yanking us off the highway. Throwing the car into park on the shoulder, I glare at him, then open my door and get out. Standing next to the field before me, in a patch of Forget-Me-Nots, I open my arms to the wide, cloudless sky.

I turn to the open passenger window, glaring at Jack who's still sitting there, gazing at me. *'Do you remember when I asked you to pull over that time when you were rushing us through Kansas? Do you? Do you know why I wanted to stand there for a few minutes and take everything in?'*

'Sure. But this isn't Kansas.'

'I know that' I reply sarcastically, my voice rising as I plow on. *'Your cost benefit analysis fucked up, Jack. This is what it always missed as you were spinning those circles in your head. It's what I forgot when I put that goddamn gun in my mouth.'*

I turn back to the open field. *'You forgot what you wrote to me during the war, Jack,'* I bellow. *'Words that kept us close and got me through that shit hole. You reminded me that happiness, life, isn't waiting for you somewhere else. It isn't waiting for you around the next bend, or over some fucking mountain. You don't have to go anywhere to find it, Jack.'* I shake my hands in the air. *'Life Jack, is right fucking here. In this moment.'*

A weighty momentary pause passes between us. I can tell he's humbled by my outburst, but I don't care. *'And Jesus fuck on a popsicle stick, Jack, I'll tell ya something else. Challenges are just fucking challenges. They're not obstacles to be avoided. Why didn't you realize that the worst experience of your life might just, just maybe, Jack, turn out to be something good? I mean, for fuck's sake, did you ever think for one goddamn minute that what you were going through could've led to something better? Like me, with the war, even after twenty years. And now, you're missing out on everything, aren't you?'*

I pause, but only to gulp in air. *'For all your fucking intellect and philosophy, Jack, you never could deliver to yourself, could you?'*

A trucker's horn blares as he zips by. He's probably confused as to why someone is standing next to his car in front of an empty field. Some absurd, crazy man shouting to himself.

I ignore him and open my eyes. After a moment, I walk around the car and get in. Back behind the wheel, I grasp it and stare straight ahead as a herd of cars whizzes by.

Chasing each other; passing each other. Each one trying to get ahead.

Sighing, I'm suddenly weary. My voice falls to a calm, even tone. Mild and pastoral. Sadness wells in the pit of my stomach as I turn to him. *'You forgot that now is now, Jack. That all things pass.'*

His eyes lock with mine and I see compassion. Regret with a sense of empathy for the pain we share, both from the past and here. Now. *'We might have had more miles together. More exits to take. More roads to explore. And you know what, Jack? You turned your back on why, in every sense of the word, we indulged in every goddamn bursting fucking moment. It wasn't about finding something or going west,'* my arms fly up, then back to the steering wheel, *'or having stuff, or this and that. Christ, whatever, man.'*

The gear lever is back in Drive now. The wheels are spinning as I pull out into the slow lane. White stripes passing below us.

Gaining speed, we're moving forward; regardless of direction.

Down the road flanked by the Forget Me Nots.

I sit back in my seat as another herd of cars passes us. *'You forgot that we were living, Jack. You forgot that, deep down, underneath all the bullshit, we knew it.'*

Interlude, Part Four – A Couch with a Blanket

A knock on the door.

I opened it with caution.

The cops.

Two tall, muscular men, their navy-blue uniforms neat and tidy, silver badges shiny, duty belts loaded with an arsenal of imposing equipment.

My stomach flipped with the actuality of jurisdiction, law, and command.

A baton. Pepper spray. A radio with a walkie-talkie mouthpiece clipped to their shoulder straps. A pistol in a holster. Theirs look like Glocks. They have spare magazine pouches too.

My dry throat felt an urge to talk shop about their weapons.

"Ev'ning. We got a call from a friend of yours. She said you might be having a rough night and thinking about ending your life. Can we speak with you for a few minutes?"

○

"Are you having any more thoughts or feelings about suicide tonight?" the hospital psychologist asked.

"Nope. I'm done with that," I replied, thirsty now to get out of authoritative possession. "Absolutely done. No more. Vamoose. Finis, as they say,"

A moment of pause.

Her pencil checked a box on a form. The form went into a file folder. She then leaned back in her squeaky, padded swivel chair.

I winced with unease.

"I certainly hope not. Suicide is never the answer. But if you feel you're safe to go home, is there anyone you can call to come get you?"

"Yeah," I told her. "There's Jack. My best friend. He lives up in Denver."

"Do you feel able to do that?"

My blurry mind had cleared somewhat from the booze and pot, my thoughts more coherent after three or four hours in the emergency room. The cops had watched over me while I sobered up and waited for the hospital shrink to finish with another late-night visitor to UCHealth Memorial Hospital Central. Listened to me patiently as I ranted and raved about the war, waved my arms about as I told them about the bombings, the gunfire, families being gunned down, soldiers who were kidnapped, politicians who played games with lives, the endless daily pounding of mortar attacks.

My divorce.

Stood by calmly as I paced around the single room and yelled about how my soul had been wrenched from my body; torn into shavings of dust. Dust that was lost forever in the deserts of Iraq. They even helped me put my hospital gown on correctly after I put it on backwards, their grins barely concealed as they informed me my balls were hanging out. With a firm grasp, they sat me down and I dangled my feet over the edge of the hospital bed, my dazed, bland eyes squinting in the glare of fluorescent overhead lights.

A feeble thanks was all I could manage.

Now, opposite the woman with stale coffee breath and dark bags under eyes, a stunning contrast to her immaculate bleach blonde hair tucked neatly in a loose bun, I felt worn out, exhausted of energy. My mind finally drained of post-traumatic stress and ready for sleep. My stomach grumbled with queasy hunger. I burped up some bile and quickly covered my mouth as I mumbled, "I can do that."

"It's been a very long night for you. I suggest getting some rest. Things will seem brighter in the morning. They always do. Why don't you try reaching out to him so he can come pick you up? I'm sure he won't mind." Then to the officer who waited slouched against her office door frame, hands hooked into his utility belt. "Sean, would you show this young man to the phone, please."

I could feel the banal pity as it emanated from her lips.

I gathered my hospital gown around my backside. As I did so, she reached for the next folder from the stack on her desk.

O

"You scared the fuck out of me tonight, Dana. I mean, I was worried before. Borderline scared. But now, I've crossed over."

"I'm sorry, Jack. I really am."

"What made you think of doing this? You have too much to live for."

"I don't know. I guess I just reached the end. Just couldn't do it anymore."

"Do what?"

"Live."

"Pardon me, but that's just fucking crazy." He thought for a moment, his face bunched up in one of his scowls. "This is probably one of the stupidest things you've ever done, Dana. You can do anything in this life. Anything. You're smart, you're sensitive – you have good insight. Talent. Jesus, man."

"You don't understand."

"Well, you're right about that. I don't. Life is too precious to go fuckin' around with it like you did. If anything, that asshole war should've taught you that much."

I sighed. My head hurt. A throb against the front of my skull. "It also taught me that life and death don't matter very much."

The familiar scoff from pursed lips as he sat down next to me.

I wiggled my legs to make room.

"Balarky," he muttered.

Groggy irritation flashed through me. Irritation at being lectured to by someone who never went to war; never understood what it was like to have the sidewalk pulled out from under his feet as everything he had built crashed around him.

Self-pity didn't allow me to see that maybe he did understand. That maybe he could help me. That maybe he was helping me and being a friend. Showing me love through his anger. But my mind was too fuzzy to play connect the dots. Prone and stretched out on my couch, a blanket that Jack had gotten from my bedroom air mattress wrapped around me, my mind was already half in a dream state. I settled back into my couch a little more, my body thankful to finally be lying down.

"You didn't have to come pick me up, you know."

"Of course I had to. I wasn't about to leave you stranded in some hospital."

"And I don't need your pity," I growled.

He glanced at the empty wall of my apartment for a second, then back at me. "I'm not pitying you. I'm reminding you. You lived through that monstrous Hell for a reason. Don't waste it."

"What reason?"

"Some other time." He looked around, like a spy who scouts for the unseen. "So, if I go home, you're not going to do anything dumb, are you? Do I have to remove all the knives from the kitchen or something?"

"You're leaving?"

He looked at his watch; a military analog with an olive drab strap. "Dude, I have to. It's three thirty. By the time I get back to Denver, it'll be just about time for me get up to go to work."

Eyes closed, I let my head flop sideways. "Okay. That's cool. But Jack?"

"What?"

"I never intended for any of this. I was – I was just searching for direction. I just wanted to do somethin' good. Have purpose and feel needed. You know?"

"I know. Now go to sleep."

He pulled the blanket up under my chin and, as he held his hand on my chest for a moment, I felt a slight tremble. Then, he got up, switched off the boob lamp in the ceiling, and walked to the door of my apartment. Turning, he said, "I love you, my brother. Sleep well."

I heard the door close softly as my eyes fluttered shut.

○

The next morning, when I awoke, I barely remembered the day before, even the cops. I stared into the bathroom mirror for a long time. How long, I don't know. The minutes didn't matter as I searched my eyes, tried to recognize something of myself through the bloodshot, dark, puffy, baggy bulges underneath.

The grey skin of my face.

I was afraid I might as well be looking at a picture of a friend. A one-time celebrity. Someone I saw in line at a convenience store. But the fear was muted by detachment. The same old ghostly feeling of being removed from my body. My mind. And that made me panicky. Here isn't real.

The blue of my eyes looked faded. Cold and vacant and dead.

And I broke down, cried again. I sank to my knees, the floor cold to my skin, and leaned against the rim of the fiberglass tub as I cradled my face in my hands. Racked by convulsive sobs. A half-hour passed and when my tear ducts ran out, I slumped back against the bathtub, hands limp on the tile floor, bankrupt of energy.

I have to do something, I thought. *Anything. Just take one fucking step.*

The only way out was to drop my cynicism. It was too easy to run around, angry and lashing out. Swimming, treading, sinking, and drowning in pain. Easier, but not the way to live. Hard roads yield the best results. And I had a choice to make.

A simple decision—live or not live.

I began to laugh. I laughed because I wasn't afraid anymore. I wasn't afraid because I knew then that death was always an option.

I had nothing more to prove.

Nothing to lose by staying alive.

The soldier got to his feet.

Mirror, Mirror

I'm past Chicago, a city that's wretched to drive through, whatever time of day is chosen. And this afternoon certainly wasn't an exception, wasn't opportune with the combination of heavy traffic and ongoing construction throughout. Lane shifting. Closed lanes.

And of course, the typical push and shove of merging.

The windy city. Some say the nickname is a badge of honor reflecting its resilience and energy. Some say it comes from the talkative nature of its citizens. Or its mix of charm and toughness.

Whatever your belief, for me, it's just plain cold.

It's also the home of Al Capone. Former home, should I say. The infamous gangster who, like the Kennedys, made money providing liquid relief to those in need of escaping their lives and their unrealized, broken dreams. Losers and winners. Gangsters and presidential families.

All different, yet the same.

But I'm close to another border on this second day of driving. Indiana, then Ohio. Closer to being home. Much calmer now, my mood softened after my release in Iowa, I light a cigarette and turn to Jack. *'I have more to say.'*

Jack arches his back from the empty passenger seat and yawns. Deep and sustained. Nonchalant, like a bear beginning to stir from winter hibernation. He yawns, then turns to me. *'What's on your mind?'*

My eyes wander over the view. Two stretches of highway. Mirrors of the other but with the same miles of flat and grass. The same signs. The same exits, but merely going in different directions.

Nothing more.

Here we go again.

'Question. Despite the irony of you shooting yourself, has it ever occurred to you that we have a lot of parallels between us?' I ask.

'Answer with a question. You mean aside from growing up in sucky alcoholic families and trying to get away from the past,' he answers.

A family in a minivan passes us, father and mother silent, and intent on the road in front of them. I spot two young children in the back seats, indulging in their screen time.

I take a deep drag off my cigarette as a jarring, blurry memory of throwing a lounge chair across the living room of my apartment shoots through me. *'Yeah.'*

'I have.'

The pounding of Jack's sledgehammer, the crashing of cabinets splintering on the kitchen floor, echoes in my ears.

'So the morning after you tore apart the kitchen with the sledgehammer, you must have been asking the same questions I did. Who is this scary motherfucker in the mirror? This can't be me. What am I doing?'

'I was.'

Like my own, Jack's naked display of rage was, and still is, terrifying. Fueled by alcohol or not, the sledgehammer and the lounge chair were howls from within. Self-loathing rage sprung from within hearts confused as to why no one understood our pain. The onslaught of a haunting past or the death of a myth.

All the unfulfilled promises.

'I know you, Jack. All that guilt must have been overwhelming. I know it was for me.'

I see him passed out on the couch with the baby sleeping nearby.

'It really was, Dana.'

Now, I smell smoke from the kitchen of my apartment. From the afternoon I passed out on my own couch while a corned beef brisket boiled on the stove. The water long gone; it had begun to burn, and I woke to the acrid stench of a fire about to light.

I could've killed someone.

But perfectly flawed, I'm just like Jack. And Jack is like me. Filled with consistency and contradiction. Resignation and determination. Doubt and conviction. And replete with successes, failures, passions, dislikes, strengths, and faults. And fears. Two out of control losers with no hope of redemption. Hopeless and afraid. Lost in the tattered remains of a life.

'We were afraid because there was no balance within us,' he says. *'That came from self-neglect. From not honestly confronting our reflections, therefore we never found harmony.'*

'Question. Do you think I'm slowly, maybe, finding a little balance?'

'Answer. I do. And you have. The war gave you more than you realize, Dana. Because the irony of hard experience is that you were honest about what you went through. You learned what it had to teach, and you began to see from an entirely different perspective. In that way, like this trip, you made meaning from looking into the mirror.'

He looks out over the landscape. *'I can't speak for anyone but for me. I couldn't find the harmony that I needed in my reflection, so there weren't any options. It was that plain and simple.'*

I turn and look deeply into his eyes. *'I get that. I've felt for a long time now that I'm largely incompatible with this world, the way I see it, the way I approach it. It makes me the oddball and can be such a lonely place sometimes. So, I get that for you too. But it hurts to feel like I was never there for you when you needed me. Not at the end of your life, not when Chris died, when your Dad died, or even when we were kids. All the times I didn't step up to help you.'*

We pass through a bend in the highway, then back to the straightness. *'And you know what's worse? You wouldn't let me. I would've dropped everything, absolutely fucking everything without hesitation, if you just told me what was going on.'*

My voice begins to break. Again, tears begin to well in the corners of my eyes. I feel like I'm falling deeper into the driver's seat. Sinking and shriveling. *'If you would've just let me, Jack. If only you would've let me.'*

Jack shakes his head. *'There was nothing you could've done. They were my decisions to make and my battles to face. Just like our fathers made their own decisions.'*

He looks back out over the flat Illinois landscape. *'Besides which, you know by now that a lot of life is in how you approach an event, not the actual event itself. And you never approached anything with the intent to injure me.'*

He pauses, as if my question jogged something else within his mind. *'Question. Then you're not angry with me anymore?'*

'Answer. Not really. Actually Jack, deep down I have a lot of compassion for what you did. And I know that I wasn't thinking of you when I put the barrel in my mouth, so how can I not understand?' I glance at him. *'And I get the despair; the fuckin' rage.'*

How could I not?

'No one wants to see that reflection.' He chuckles. *'Our lives are so funny, Dana. Some things intersect so elegantly, others collide so terribly. You never know where the crack in the mirror will appear. And like me, you've been avoiding the hard part. For you, the hardest part of this journey.'*

'What's that, Jack?'

Ignoring my question, he returns his gaze to the open window, at the passing canvas of the Earth. Barron to some. Rich with life to others.

He sighs. *'I wish I had a roast beef sub. I'm starved.'*

'I hate to break it to you Jack, but you can't eat,' I tell him with a laugh.

'Yeah, it's kind of a bummer, because as much as needs may change, desires never cease.'

In the Haunted Museum

Hazy today, but I'm still pushing hard. I'm exhausted and I don't want to drive anymore. Those precious few winks at the rest stop the night before, somewhere around Nebraska and Iowa, weren't enough. And my hands are trembling from road jitters—a symptom of too many miles behind the wheel.

But I can't stop.

Something's propelling me as I'm once again in

THE HEART OF IT ALL

Where I-80 merges with I-90 and becomes a state turnpike. I haven't been on this stretch of highway in a while, so I'm not surprised that it's auto tolled now. I don't know when that happened. I'm only sure that it's been that way since Covid swept through the country. Times change despite any resistance. But I'm thankful the traffic's been light. Some semis delivering their goods to unknown parts. A few cars, probably commuters who caved to paying the state in favor of expediency.

And with the stereo turned off, the atmosphere in the car's been muffled as well. I still have no desire to listen to the Dead, or *Morcheeba*, or Jimmy Buffett—or any of the music Jack and I typically listened to during our trips. I'm not sure why yet. Only that the silence brings forth a sense in me that I'm paused somehow. Paused without distraction. Jack hasn't seemed to mind. He's been reclined in the passenger seat with his eyes closed, apparently as content as I to let the miles go silently by.

Distant with thought, I wipe the bleariness from my eyes and lean back in my own seat. In the depths of my tired mind, I realize that to press play, I must accept the idea of never knowing how long Jack planned the day. Or what the day was like. Or what his feelings were.

If anything earthly mattered.

And I need to look for a motel. A place to rest and sleep; a place to find some peace.

I'll also never know what the drive was like. If he saw that people around him were fulfilling their dreams and desires. And he couldn't. If he saw them appreciating the smallest of daily moments. And he didn't. I'll never know when he decided to kill himself. Six months before. Weeks before. Right there behind the wheel.

I see an exit for a Country Inn, but it's not time to stop yet.

But more importantly, I'll never know why he could be in a place yet was never truly there. Why he didn't find a place where his identity felt at home. Where his heart was still, at ease within that haven. And why, even though he expounded on theories of spiritual freedom, why he doubted himself, and struggled to apply them to construct a life worth living.

Sheltered from fear, chaos, and pain.

I'll never know why he couldn't find lasting happiness within the stereotypical life he had. Or why he couldn't be happy without the motion; the momentary, forward momentum of life on the road as he forever attempted to outrun the sun.

I'll never know why he couldn't perceive the cost of logic and the benefit of self-compassion. Or even why he didn't reach out to talk with me. To trust and confide in me. To ask for help, reassurance, and comfort. Because I know that he couldn't take down the

ENTRY FORBIDDEN

sign nailed to the door of his heart.

The sun winks at me through the rearview mirror as it begins to flicker on the horizon.

And I'll never know his final thought. Or if it was cut off in mid—

Crack.

I pass by exit 187. The Streetsboro exit. My eyes linger on it as it passes. If I was to take it, I'd be heading south toward Kent State, a university forever haunted by its own turn at a trigger.

Back to the road.

I also know that if he had reached out to me, and if I had been able to help him, that he might just have gone ahead with killing himself anyway. In the face of that kind of determination, how could I have realistically stopped him?

My eyes are burning, itchy, and red as they squint into the mirror. The sun is setting fast. Heading in this direction, there is no way to outrun the sun.

I also know that I have his ashes. I know that I will keep his ashes. I want to keep them because they're a necessary reminder for me to keep repeating, *Yes, he's really dead, Dana. This isn't a dream. This isn't some absurd figment of your imagination*, because I know that I will never feel the reality of his death fully enough.

And I know that, regardless, I will always live with the questions, *Could I have saved him? Somehow? Someway? Could I have returned the favor?* That no matter how much I contemplate his death, no matter how much I try to understand and integrate it into my heart, he will be with me forever.

No miles can erase our life together. Our journey can't be milled and repaved. No matter which way I turn, which road I take, I will always come back to the haunted museum of our life.

I'm exhausted with the road. I must stop. I'm ready to stop, but I can't.

Not quite yet.

'So Jack, final question. And I need an answer. Please. From the bottom of my heart I need to know this.'

He opens his eyes, sits up straight, and turns to me.

I look at him, hoping he's appreciating the gravity of my coming question. He is. I can tell by the concentration in his eyes. His steadfast attention. As he's always given to our friendship.

'I want to know why I lived, and you didn't.'

And for the first in our life together, I see him waver, his logic and intelligence groping for an answer. He looks helpless but acquiescing as he reaches out and grips my shoulder. His hand feels firm and honest, yet warm and tender. *'I'm sorry, Dana, but truthfully, after all I've learned in all the books I've scoured, after all my travels and after all I've tried, succeeded at, failed at, and experienced, I haven't a fucking clue. But you need to understand that you were supposed to live for a reason. And as much as you may not want to, I need you to look into the mirror and be at ease with one inevitable, excruciating truth – that life is about perpetual uncertainty. Regardless of our predilection toward them, there are no answers to any of this. And there never will be.'*

We look at each other in the fading light. A shared moment beyond friendship as we both accept what is.

What has to be.

The Other Side of the Maple Tree

There's a man standing in what seems to be a pasture. Maybe a prairie; vast and open. A space with deep green grass that stretches over rugged, snowcapped mountains to beyond infinity. Into a swirly Van Gogh interstellar heaven that's outlandishly deep blue, with hints of tangerine, blush, and lemon.

A large, hot ball hovers above. It glimmers in the dark, wet umber mud that's smeared on the tips of the man's desert Army combat boots. The ball's hurting his eyes. Pain, like the deserts of Iraq.

White light. Thick heat.

Before him, there's a stone wall, circular and broken. Still being built; a pile of rocks in a corner never placed. Bright leaves are scattered on the ground; a kaleidoscope—russet, golden bronze, purplish red, and light tan. And the wind is blowing. Twirling, swirling tawny sand around his ankles. But his hair doesn't move. The leaves don't move either. In the center of the wall, there's a maple tree. Thick bark, gnarled, with black bands running up and down.

A figure slides out from the other side of the tree; a syrupy silhouette lazily forming. Gelatinous with no color. Getting taller until he sees what it is. A T-shirt. Nondescript. But decorated with little patches—gold arrowheads and Webelos. Blue jeans and hiking boots.

Nervous. Queasy and unsteady.

A face emerges. He can see it and his stomach twists. He needs to go to him, his body moving on its own.

Why is he afraid?

Closer. The figure is smiling. Happy.

Overwhelmed with desperate impulse, the man lunges at the figure. Arms thrown around him, hugging tightly. Squeezing his upper back.

Can't let go. Can't let go. Can't. Terrified to let go.

He wants so badly to be with this figure. This man; his friend.

Over the figure's shoulder, he murmurs, "Oh my God, I've missed you. Missed you so very much. So much. Tell me, please, tell me, where have you been?"

The figure pulls back, hands grasping upper arms. "Dana?" he asks, his gray/blue eyes bright and shining.

And empty arms close in on one another. A futile embrace of the man's own shoulders. Of himself. Closing in tighter and tighter until his shoulders ache and his fingers cramp. He lets go, his limp, helpless hands dropping to his waist, one weighted with a pistol. His eyes are clamping shut with a single shot.

Crack.

An ungodly, penetrating echo.

The man jolts upright, breathless, wide eyes searching the protracted dark corners of the hotel room. A Comfort Inn. A few moments pass until he realizes he's not home yet; that he's still on the road.

The third day of driving.

I take a deep breath and wipe the sweat off my brow with the corner of a sheet. A moment later, I taste the bitter gun oil on my lips as I slide out from the sheets and sit on the edge of the bed. My shoulders slumped; my elbows resting on my knees.

I'm weary even though I've slept.

My belly growls. It's been growling for days but it feels like weeks. Months. Sometime today I'm going to stop for a sub; an overly stuffed foot-long hero sandwich. Maybe roast beef with everything on it. And I realize that for the first time, in a very long time, I'm starving. But not just for food.

I want to be reverent and ravenous.

I want to be spirited for life again.

The Deepest Part of Sadness

On the east side of Pennsylvania, close to the New York border, I'm dashing by the lapping waters of the Susquehanna River. The lucent water cutting through the mountains, rushing through the hills and valleys, then gently slowing when it gets to the open lands; breaking when the landscape beckons it to. Forever flowing. Somewhere to somewhere. Unknown, but with purpose.

With a dense, white, early morning fog wrapped around me, I round a bend in the highway, and the exit for Promised Land State Park emerges. From blurry to clear as I'm passing it, like a camera lens focusing. After just a moment, it's in the rearview mirror, rapidly fading into the mist.

I'll be in New York soon and I'm absorbed within the tranquility of the morning. I'm also enjoying the cool air flowing through the window; cool with a hint of dew.

My home stretch morning. The dim air signals earthy sleeping in.

And I'm crying.

Now.

Alone.

Oh, dear God, I miss my friend.

I miss when he would talk for fifteen minutes about how chain restaurants were garbage and not worth going to because you were only feeding a corporation instead of yourself. How a local restaurant offered more charismatic flavor, and better food, not to mention helping mom and pop put food on their own table.

I miss when he would insist that we get off the highway to take back roads because of the experience, telling me that we never saw anything interesting on the highway, just the same old repetitious monotony of the same old commercial America. How he would never take the same road twice.

I miss how he would always say he knew a shortcut. Jack's famous shortcuts to the bar when we were living in Denver. Shortcuts which would inevitably lead us to somewhere entirely unplanned, unthought of—and two hours later than promised.

I miss how he would crank up the stereo in our apartment's living room, as much as it grated on my nerves at the time. *Morcheeba* resonating through the walls while he puttered around, occupying himself in every moment. Sitting still meant wasting valuable time.

And I miss how he would travel endless circles in his mind, his own logic defying even him, as he thought everything through. Weighing the cost/benefit analysis of any kind of situation or philosophy.

Oh, dear God, I miss my friend.

I miss him so very much.

I reach for the blueberry muffin I snagged from the hotel's continental breakfast bar. Shaking from starvation, my emotions, and from being on the road, I rip open the plastic wrapper with my teeth.

Why didn't I appreciate those moments more? Why didn't I try to memorize them? To engrave them, indelible, in every part of my mind. To put them in sacred spaces. So close there would never be a chance of letting them go. Why didn't I understand how precious they were? Why did I take such advantage of time? We didn't have as much as I thought.

I ease my foot off the accelerator, slowing to sixty-five miles per hour.

And I must admit something, here in the privacy of my car, where no one can hear me or see me, where I won't have to be put on display. I never had the courage to tell Jack how much he meant to me; how profoundly he changed my life for the better; how he taught me to live more fully. Or how much fun I had with him; how deeply I needed and wanted him with me; how I admired his spirit. Or how much I regretted that the war and my post-traumatic behavior separated us; how radically those events haunted me; how they left me lonely without him. How much he was a part of my heart. My soul. Too afraid to express the words.

Now down to sixty miles per hour.

Without the distraction of wolfing down the muffin, I'm weeping again. Deep, belly churning, I-never-know-where-or-when-sobs. And while I don't believe they will ever subside completely, they have eased. Slowly diminishing, like my anger. More of a quiet thrum now. A vibration that will always live in my heart.

I've been crying because of regret born from belated cognizance. Because I must admit that I couldn't tell Jack I loved him when we were in Moab. I was too self-conscious. Too immature within my masculinity. Too fearful of rejection, judgment, or scorn.

But these are only my thoughts. Sitting next to the 'Jack in a Box,' I'm left to contemplate them alone, in the deepest part of my sadness.

I wipe my nose on the sleeve of my T-shirt, blink my way through another bend in the highway, and crest a hill. The landscape opens, offering me a breathtaking view of the rolling hills. I smile and breathe in deeply.

Fifty-five miles per hour.

I've needed this. This time. This space on the road. But as much as I've appreciated the space and time to reflect on Jack, with Jack, about our friendship, our life together, and his loss, I want to be off the road. And as much as I'm going to savor these last moments, I know now that, like the main character in *Coming Up for Air*, even though I've longed to stay in these places, I can't stay stuck in the past.

The fog of the promised land is behind me and I'm ready. I'm ready to be home. Where I now choose to spend my time.

There's no need to rush anymore.

No need to run.

The crystal, golden morning bathes me, coloring my face with the light of a new day as I'm driving toward the sun.

Our Hearts & Minds

Dee takes a sip of his coffee, then grimaces. "Don't ever get coffee from Wendy's. It's the absolute worst." Another sip; another grimace. "Just terrible. Let that be a warning to you; to all of mankind." He looks down at the picnic table. A finger toys with the wood, picking and scratching.

We're back at the meandering stretch of piled rock, after walking the long asphalt footpath with the view of the New England hills surrounding it, and past the small regional airport and the few designated walking trails cutting through tangled brambles with dead ends. Now we're sitting on the picnic table at the end of the levee that ends with the skull of a dam, where the reservoir still is. Still in check and pooled. The clusters of green forest that still cling to the slopes and blanket the horizon—oaks, maples, and birch—have yet to begin turning color.

The warmth of the early autumn air drifts over this hometown levee. And over us.

Change, but no change.

I laugh. "Jack used to say that the road to Hell is paved with decaf coffee grounds."

He looks up at me. "This isn't decaf. But I agree."

"He also called sugar, the white death."

Dee smiles. "I remember being over at Jack's when we were

all young and his mom making dinner. Loved the smell of that kitchen – until after the divorce." He pauses, then chuckles. "Carl was a terrible cook. I remember, one time, seeing the cats eating out of the pot of chili on the stove. At least they liked it."

A glutton for punishment, he takes another sip of his coffee. "I've never met a more unique family. You know, Jack told me one time that his father died from a disease that he got from one of the cats?"

I look at him, befuddled. I'm not sure what to make of this revelation.

A final twist to the saga.

And I know now, beyond any shadow, that, even after a lifetime, I'll never know the whole story of Jack. After all that I've pondered, speculated, tried to settle, or even closed, I'll never solve the mystery of him.

Or any human.

But I'm also sure there's one more thing I have to do.

"Seriously, man? That's not what he told me."

"I'm not sure it really matters anymore."

I sigh. "I guess not."

"You never could tell with him if what he was telling you, about anything personal, was real or not. I'm not sure why, only that maybe he was not dealing with it himself."

"That's probably true. Jack was a master avoider when it came to himself. He gave more to others, more to me, than to himself."

"Are you still angry with him?" Dee asks.

Clasping my hands together, I rest my chin on them. Then, after a moment, I reply, "No. No, I'm not. He made his choice, and I understand why. I know what it's like to be in that pit. Believe me, I do. I really have no choice but to respect that."

"How?"

"Well, let me put it this way. I respect that he decided to die on his own terms. He made his own decision. It wasn't made by some doctor he didn't know or while he was staring at some wall in someplace he didn't want to be at, existing but not really living. Do I wish he was still here? Yes. But he lived and died the way he wanted to. I think there's a lot to be said for that. And you know what?"

"What?"

"I think his death is a reminder to me; a reminder that, good or bad, life and death is worth living for all that it is. It's all one big package that makes us who we are. The truth of our existence. That's not so bad."

"I'm not angry with him anymore either. I guess, in the end, we have to focus on the living, Dana. From now on, he will have to live in our hearts and minds," says Dee, his voice wistful.

"And on the page," I reply.

"Oh? Have you been writing?"

"I have. I'm just about finished with my latest book."

"And it's about him?"

"Yep. I wanted to write it. I needed to write it. I needed to write about us and to give him the honor and dignity he deserves."

"I think that's great. Has it been cathartic in any way?"

I shrug. Not casually or apathetically, but more with a feeling of ambivalence. "I'm not sure how to answer that, to be honest," I reply, my mind trying to process an answer. "I mean, logistically, it's been a tough one. Just the sheer amount of material. All the years. The memories. But about the feelings…"

"Really hard to get through?"

"Yeah. I guess I would have to say yes and no." I pause and look out over the forest, and into the wilderness of the heart. "My gut says that's the way it will always be."

Dee's eyes become lost in thought for a moment. "Maybe by writing, you can start to let go of him. You know you have to, right?"

"Have you?"

He nods. "I have."

"Well, I think you're right. I mean, yeah. I guess. I think I'm starting to. I guess that's all I can say right now."

"Can't wait to read it."

I chuckle. "You should. You're in it."

Dee's eyes twinkle with happiness. "I am?"

"You sure are. But I have to change your name. Got anything in mind?"

"Let me think on it."

"Cool."

He returns to toying with the splinter of wood nestled in the swirled grain of the picnic table. A small pry of his fingers, and he stares at it, then hands it to me.

I twirl the splinter between my own fingers, then gently place it on the table. Back where it was. Entwined, reunited with the grain.

Intuitively, we both get up and stretch.

Time to start walking. Time to go home. Time to begin moving forward with our lives.

I turn to him as we trudge along. "I'm glad you're in my life. I don't have much of a family. Well, no one really. No grandparents; they're all dead. My mom's dead. Jack's dead. And, when my father dies, I'll be alone. Like truly alone."

"No, you won't. You'll always have me. I'm your family now."

We hug in the

Relics

parking lot before parting ways.

Dee gets into his car and looks at me. He has a serious, matter of fact, plain, simple expression on his face. "I'm glad you're back."

"Me too. I'm kinda done with this whole east west thing."

He shrugs. "East. West. Doesn't really matter where you are, as long as you're fully there."

He starts his car.

"Wanna hit a Folf course next week?" I ask.

"If the weather's good, yeah. Sounds like great fun. Let me know when you want to."

"Roger that."

I stop typing and review the last chapter I've written. My conversation with Dee, which took place only two weeks ago.

One year has passed since I came home; home to my familiar stomping grounds.

The borough amid New England's hills and forest. The hamlet with neighbors who wave and mow their lawns. Who wash their cars and walk their dogs. Home to my childhood house on the winding road. With the swamp in the back woods. And the tall, bushy Rhododendron out front—big, ruffled white blooms with little stalks capped in yellow.

Where Jack and I spent so much time—sleepovers, birthday parties, cub scout meetings with snipe hunts, movies, and backyard campouts. Where we talked for hours about our imagined dreams. And where I received the phone call of his suicide and began this journey.

I'm back home with the ghosts.

But now, as I sit in front my laptop finishing this book, the house is bright and sunny. The open window breathing in a fresh autumn breeze of color turning leaves. The trees have been shedding their old growth, with new buds waiting on the branches for the coming spring.

I can smell it.

A comforting scent of revitalization.

Another change of season.

But as I mentioned to Dee, it's been a difficult book to write. Laborious and taxing to my psyche. An arduous process of not only the logistics of story craft, but of reaching deep within myself to excavate my heart.

How do I sum up Jack's character and our adventures with the rich texture they both deserve? Or the infinite depth in which friendship resides?

In which love resides.

A lifetime crammed into bulging pockets.

I look down at my computer's keyboard. The infinite possibilities contained in the letters, the words, and the choices I've made.

How do I write the end?

'You've done alright, Dana,' says Jack.

Allowing me to work, he's been quiet up until now, leaning against the half-open window which overlooks the backyard. Gazing at the lawn and forest beyond.

I turn down the classical music I've been listening to. My latest CD—Masters of the Baroque. *'Thanks, Jack. But how do I finish it?'*

He turns and takes a deep breath. *'We need to talk, Dana, while we still have the time.'*

Leaning back in my creaky, antique wooden desk chair, I smile. As always, he has my attention. *'I'm listening.'*

He smiles back. A peaceful smile stretched with nostalgia. His voice is wistful as he looks out the window again. *'You know, it's pretty crazy, huh, being here, looking out over that backyard? Full circle, man. I can still remember us tenting back there, snipe hunting and setting the woods on fire. We were so young.'*

I nod. *'I know. It is crazy. Half the time, I can hardly believe it.'*

'Me too.' He pauses. *'Are you okay?'*

'I'm sad, Jack.'

'Why?'

'Because a lot of it feels like it's fading. The memories aren't as sharp anymore. Sometimes they feel so distant, as if I can't reach them. And that sucks, Jack. I just wish I had a rewind button or maybe a DVD to watch.'

'That's natural, man, but here's the deal. Some of the images may fade, but not the feeling. The feelings in your heart stay forever.'

He turns, looks at me, and I see his face—alive, healthy, vibrant—in the golden rays of the new morning. Eyes soft and gentle. *'And it's of your heart that we need to talk about. Do you remember when we were kids, and we used to swing together on the playground?'* he asks.

'I do. So?'

'You're still on them.'

'Say what?'

'The playground and the swings. They can mean many different things as we go through life, but I think, right now, for you, they mean letting go and getting back to the basics.'

'What basics?'

'Swinging is simple joy, Dana. You need to lighten up about things. Let that little boy get out and about and play.'

'Just what are you getting at, Jack?'

He looks back out the window deep, into the woods. Then, back to me. *'You took the gun out of your mouth, Dana. I didn't. And because you made that decision, live fully, don't just suffer through it. Make it conform to you, rather than letting yourself conform to it. You, and only you, decides the cog you want to be, let alone if it matches a socket. But whatever happens, don't beat yourself up or think you're worthless like I did. You'd be wasting your decision.'*

He pauses and frowns. A stern affirmation. *'You know all this, Dana. You've had this figured out for a long time. When you were coming home from the war. When you were walking the levee. I'm only reinforcing, reminding you of these notions. And you've taken some great steps forward toward actualizing them. You're a writer now. Full blown. Tried and true. But what you need to do now is find it in your heart to go further. To keep taking steps. To go further, Dana. You should know by now that life is way too short to do otherwise.'*

I nod as all his words bring comfort to my heart. A warmth that begins to radiate outward into my entire body.

My eyes take in the sun—a bright, circular aura filtering through the glass. I close them and breathe deeply of the fresh air from the late autumn breeze.

One more chapter to write and this book will be finished. It will be time to start packing up the artifacts that surround me.

I need to put away my father's antique clock collection, including the one he gave me for my birthday. The brass airplane propeller paperweight. Pictures of him in Korea. And of us when I was young—birthdays, vacations, holidays.

And of Jack as well.

I need to pack up his road sign. The button down shirt he wore, then handed down to me. The books he gave me. The Grateful Dead we listened to.

I need to put away his journal.

And his ashes.

Without me realizing it, these scraps of the past have convened; grown in my studio over the months while I wrote. Bit by bit. Piece by piece. They cover my bookcase. They're propped up here and there on the shelves. Nestled by the window. The clocks on the floor around me. The road sign leaning against a spare chair.

And I know now that I needed them with me while I was writing. They helped me reach the memories again; encouraged me to feel the little boy again.

Especially Jack.

I needed his presence. His advice. His nod of approval. He provided the courage, the determination, and the insight I needed to tell our stories. I needed him to overcome the numbness; to move through and comfort my gut tumbles of sadness, regrets, and doubts. The heaviness which mentally exhausted me as the pages accumulated. But also to relive and share the joy and happiness of being with him.

The bonds which have never left me.

That, in all likelihood, never will.

But while I have no desire to throw these fragments of evidence, these keepsakes of a life lived, in a heap of trash at my town's dump, it's time to stop lingering in a shrine of the past; stop living among the relics from the dead.

I once asked Jack what a sense of failure might be, and he replied that a sense of failure is not being able to imagine anymore. When you forget who you are.

But unlike George Bowling in *Coming Up for Air*, I know now that failure is also not integrating the past, present, and future as the sum of what makes up me. And sitting here, finding peace with my life, with Jack, I also know that he's right.

My destination is not about being able to go home, as it were. It's not a matter of place. Rather, it's a different way of being. It's a sense of inner quietude fixed from comfort; comfort in knowing that it's okay to continually reinvent myself, experience new ideas, and ultimately to do what I want with my life.

To not be dictated by spectral hauntings, mandates, sadness, regret, or escape.

I look up and see Jack standing next to me. He puts his hand on my shoulder and smiles. It's warm and radiant, soothing and loving. *'I think I'll take a walk in the woods.'*

'You're leaving, aren't you?'

'Yes.'

'Do you have to?'

'It's time, Dana. I have to go. And to answer your question, you end this book, this chapter and journey of your life, by letting go and moving forward while being in the moment. Because you're awake, and now it's time to keep your eyes open.'

'Where're you goin'?'

He shrugs. *'Doesn't much matter, does it?'*

He turns, puts his hands in his pockets and strolls to the door of my studio.

Casual.

Timeless.

Not a care in the world.

And I know I need to tell him. To tell him now. Before this moment is lost in a private space of no return or sharing.

'I love you, Jack.'

Stopping, he turns back to me. *'I love you too.'*

Then he walks through the doorway of my studio.

I listen to his footsteps echoing on our childhood stairs. As they step through the living room, stride through the kitchen, cross the threshold of the back door and onto the deck; then into the grass of the yard. As they fade toward the woods beyond.

I go to the window, part the curtains, and watch until he blends with the hemlocks, the oaks, the birch.

And I can't help but smile.

I feel young.

Young again.

I watch until he's an umbra under the wide canopy of the immense sum and substance of the Earth. A silhouette merged with, and at home, with the peace of nature.

Then, he's gone.

F. Scott Service lives in New England and is an international award-winning, full-time author.

His first book, *Lines in the Sand: An American Soldier's Personal Journey in Iraq*, won a bronze medal in the 2022 Wishing Shelf Book Awards for Adult Nonfiction and was awarded the Pacific Book Review Star for a Memoir of Excellent Merit. His second, *Playing Soldier: A Chronicle of Spiritual Awakening*, won the 2021 Indie Reader Discovery Award for Memoir and also placed Finalist in the 2021 National Indie Excellence Awards for New Nonfiction, the Book Excellence Awards for Memoir, the Wishing Shelf Book Awards for Best Cover Design and Adult Nonfiction, the Independent Author Network (IAN) Book Awards for Autobiography/Biography, the N.N. Light Book Awards for Memoir, and the Honorable Mention Award in the 2021 Readers' Favorite Book Awards.

In his spare time, he gardens, tends to his Bonsai trees, plays baritone ukulele, cooks, and travels.

You may connect with him at his website: www.fscottservice.com

www.ingramcontent.com/pod-product-compliance
Lightning Source LLC
Chambersburg PA
CBHW051817090426
42736CB00011B/1515

* 9 7 9 8 9 9 3 4 8 2 2 2 4 *